Praise for
Secrets of Strong Couples

"As a matrimonial lawyer of forty years, I feel that Julie and David touched upon some very difficult subjects that couples are faced with, but they are unprepared to deal with. As a result, the issues are not discussed between them in a productive manner and can lead to acrimony in the relationship. The wonderful dynamic between this couple is remarkable—with David 'stating the obvious' (i.e., what everyone is thinking but afraid to say) in a manner that normalizes the issue; and then Julie steps in to reframe the issue so as to enlighten and teach the psychological perspective. The result: it brings hope to the couple, which is just terrific. Julie looks behind what is actually happening, and articulates the source of the problem, not what appears to be happening on the surface, so it is easier for the couple to understand and deal with. I found the chapters addressing bipolar disorder, ADHD, trans issues, and boundaries with parents particularly enlightening because parents just do not know how to deal with these topics and are ashamed to even discuss them. The Bulitts' courage in sharing their own story made me cry, but that in and of itself brings authenticity to the entire book. Well done!"

—Robin Taub, Esquire, matrimonial lawyer

"Written by a licensed relationship therapist and a divorce attorney, if you read this book, you won't need the services of either! Insightful and relatable, the stories and advice in this book can help ANY couple!"

—**Becca Anderson**, author of *Let Me Count the Ways*

"In an age of Instagram perfection and rom-com endings, David and Julie Bulitt are a wonderful breath of fresh air. *Secrets of Strong Couples* tackles the most difficult situations a couple can face—from illness, to infidelity, to the loss of a child and more. The Bulitts help each couple to share their story and how they survived, and then find the most valuable lessons for the rest of us. Honest, respectful, revealing, caring, and, above all, supremely helpful, *Secrets of Strong Couples* is a vital roadmap for how to keep lasting love in your life, no matter what life throws your way."

—**Lyric W. Winik**, *NYT* bestselling writer and coauthor of *How To Be Human: An Autistic Man's Guide to Life*

"Want to save money and avoid divorce court? The family therapist and divorce attorney, married for more than thirty-five years, provide concrete advice for everything from infidelity to adoption that affect marriages. Read both this book and their first one and you may save your marriage. It's an eye-opener!"

—**Julie Schoerke**, founder of Books Forward and Books Fluent

"This book is special. The selections are current, topical, and up to now, many are largely untouched. The takeaways are spot on! Julie and David's candor about their personal experience adds humility and real-world experience to their professional depth. It's an engaging and insightful read."

—Deborah Reiser, Esq., matrimonial lawyer, Best Lawyers in America, Lawyer of the Year 2016, 2020

SECRETS
OF
STRONG
COUPLES

SECRETS
OF
STRONG
COUPLES

Personal Stories and Couples
Communication Skills for
Long-Lasting Relationships

JULIE BULITT & DAVID BULITT

LCSW-C   JD
Family Therapist   Divorce & Family Lawyer

CORAL GABLES

For permission requests, please contact the publisher at:
Mango Publishing Group
2850 S Douglas Road, 2nd Floor
Coral Gables, FL 33134 USA
info@mango.bz

For special orders, quantity sales, course adoptions and corporate
sales, please email the publisher at sales@mango.bz. For trade
and wholesale sales, please contact Ingram Publisher Services at
customer.service@ingramcontent.com or +1.800.509.4887.

Secrets of Strong Couples: Personal Stories and Couples
Communication Skills for Long-Lasting Relationships

Library of Congress Cataloging-in-Publication number: 2023934037

ISBN: (hardcover) 978-1-68481-220-2 (paperback) 978-1-68481-296-7
(ebook) 978-1-68481-221-9

BISAC category code SOC026010, SOCIAL SCIENCE / Sociology /
Marriage & Family

To all of our couples, for having the courage to share.

TABLE OF CONTENTS

FOREWORD

I met Julie (a family therapist) and David (a divorce attorney) through a mutual friend. Once they were guests on my podcast, I learned this: they are real, authentic, and talk about things many people simply do not want to talk about (but need to talk about). They are the kind of people you want around your table. They are the kind of couple from whom we can all learn. And, for these reasons alone, *Secrets of Strong Couples* should be in every kitchen, family room, and bedroom: it is a book that comforts and challenges, while giving hope.

As a thera-coach who has helped hundreds of leaders at work and home become more human and many families navigate heartbreak, I deeply appreciate the power of connection. I especially appreciate that power when people humbly and honestly share their own journeys, foibles, and not-so-pretty parts. Julie and David Bulitt model how to do this with grace and humor. As someone who appreciates just how hard (and important) it is to do my own inner work, I love how this book outlines a clinical perspective while also providing wise takeaways. This book is readable and memorable. It gives us grist for the mill and encourages emotional honesty.

We all love a good story that shines a light on the path forward. We yearn to hear about losses and fears, because those painful moments offer growth and change. Julie and David give us just that and more in this lovely and inspiring book. By sharing the stories of couples who have struggled, they give us the gift of connection: we are not alone. Others have experienced the same pain and triumph, because it is in the scars that beauty is found.

It takes tremendous resilience to navigate the messiness found in any relationship. Doing so is not for the fainthearted but for the courageous. As we double down on our willingness to be brave, wisdom and healing manifest. As we navigate the details of life that we never scripted and never wanted, we learn about ourselves and deepen connection in healthy ways. Yet first we spend time in the dark, learning that without the mud, there is no lotus.

With the guidance of those who walk before us and hold a lantern so we can see, we come to trust there are markers along the path that we can follow. This book is one of those lanterns. Julie and David provide not just markers but also a steady hand and the benefit of their own marital challenges; they are transparent and vulnerable. Who among us does not need someone who walks with us, holds the map, and cheers us on?

Secrets of Strong Couples is designed to make the secrets of a happy marriage not so secret. In their ever-so-practical way, Julie and David talk about the things that many people do not want to talk about. Since we are only as sick as our secrets, they want us to know this: there are no secrets that get better, only more bitter. As a result, connecting and communicating with courage is their battle cry.

We all have things that we need to talk about, to own, and to uncover so we can recover. The Bulitts help us to do that. Reading their book is like sitting around the kitchen table with the best kind of friends: friends who will help you to say, "You too? I thought I was the only one."

Karen Benjack Hardwick, M.Div., MSW
Author of The Connected Leader: 7 Strategies to Empower Your True Self and Inspire Others

CHAPTER 1

Can We Learn from These Couples?

The adage "Misery loves company" dates back to the writings of the ancient Greeks, to the works of Shakespeare, and even to the Bible. The two of us took that long-held truth to heart in writing our first book, *The Five Core Conversations for Couples*. As a divorce lawyer and family therapist, it was no surprise that we had an awful lot of conversations and differences of opinion over the years. Together, we worked our way through a whirlpool of struggles—including infertility, adoption, raising a child with mental health struggles and near financial ruin. We talked about our varied vocations and how our goals for clients were so diverse. After comparing notes, many nearly illegible and written on crumpled and wadded pages stuffed into a folder, we began to see very distinct similarities between the issues discussed in Julie's therapy practice and my meetings with people considering divorce—not to mention the many talks we have had in more than thirty-five years of marriage. Those connections essentially served as a seam between a therapist's couch and a divorce lawyer's office. But the first book was not going to be framed solely around our professional observations. Its heart and soul would be more than that. It would combine our professional experiences, our own intimacies—as well as our own miseries.

Since its publication, we have received countless notes and emails expressing appreciation for the book and acknowledging our honesty and openness. Although a few people, and no doubt our kids as well, thought we shared a little too much information, the overwhelming response was one of recognition and appreciation for how much of ourselves we were willing to expose. We were "real," and folks seemed to find comfort in that.

We are hardly alone. Every relationship, every couple has a story to tell.

In some iterations of poker, players get to toss out the cards that they don't want and replace them with others from the deck. When people in relationships lay their cards on the table, they don't get replacements. They can either lose—or find a way to win.

The couples who persevere through life's most difficult trials find a way to play those cards they are dealt—together. They gather their chips and stay at the table and prepare themselves for the next hand.

In *The Five Core Conversations for Couples*, we took a broad look at the basics of successful relationships—how to identify, manage, and push through the primary quandaries that most couples face at one time or another. In these pages, the digging is deeper. We tackle issues and mine holes that many couples cannot climb out of or solve and are unable to escape.

Have you ever thought about it? How do they do it? How is it that some relationships not only survive but even thrive after a crisis, while others wither and flame out because of a bad weekend or a seemingly benign disagreement? How did Mary and John's marriage survive their son's death? Sam had an affair, yet he and Jennifer seem happier now more than ever. Even though Janice is an alcoholic as well as addicted to pain medication and has been in and out of rehab for several years, she and Joe made it through and are still together. The Thompsons have a transgender teen; Annie was open and understanding, but Jack shut down, got angry, and wouldn't talk about it. No problem. There they are—holding hands and taking nighttime walks together.

Most of us have heard the term "widow-maker" in reference to a deadly heart attack. A widow-maker can occur when the major descending artery that serves as a pipeline to the heart gets blocked and the heart stops beating. The way for cardiology patients to avoid a widow-maker is to have a bypass procedure to get the blood flowing around the blockage. Working through a traumatic injury to a relationship seems to require the same sense of urgency, the same need to find a way to bypass the issue, fix it, and move on.

The two of us thought a lot about these couples and their relationships. We wondered about all those questions and how it was that some people were able to avoid the relationship widow-maker and successfully navigate that bypass. Then we went out and did what we like to do: We talked to people. We were often saddened by the stories, but at the same time uplifted by their tenacity and courage. There also turned out to be an unexpected consequence of the many hours of conversations—they turned out to be a two-way street. Julie and I got much of what we were looking for—some insight into how these couples made it through, their relationships damaged and listing in some cases, but still afloat. And for those who shared their stories, it was often cathartic, a deep breath released. They felt better after opening up, letting it out, and telling their story.

There is pain in these pages, plenty of it. At the same time though, there is also resilience and determination. There is loyalty and courage. There is love. It is our hope that you will find comfort in these stories and experiences and the strength to push your relationship forward even in the toughest of times.

—Julie and David

CHAPTER 2

Surviving When Your Child and Grandchild Don't

Maggie and Glen sat closely on the love seat, their hands clasped tightly together. This was a familiar position for them.

"We keep close when we talk about Lisa and her baby," Glen explained.

Lisa was their youngest daughter. She and her unborn child were brutally murdered by Lisa's boyfriend in an isolated field. In addition to the horrible death, Maggie and Glen had to endure the agonizing search for her body and the wait for the police to investigate and charge the boyfriend.

Looking at Maggie, Glen smiled. "We have always connected through our faith. That was part of what first attracted me. It sounds corny, but it really was love at first sight," he recounted.

The middle of three girls, Maggie was born overseas and raised in a military family.

"We spent a lot of time at missions, with kids who did not have both of their parents, who were poor," Maggie said. "My parents had a deep faith and dedication to each other. They were married for over sixty years. I learned a lot from them."

The couple met when Maggie was in nursing school, having been introduced by one of Glen's previous girlfriends.

"I did not know if he would be interested in me," Maggie remembered. "He was so confident, smart, good looking."

"We had a lot in common," Glen said. "Both of us had traveled extensively when we were young, and as I said, we each had a strong faith in Jesus. Maggie is much shier and more reserved than I am. I tend to be more outgoing and more of a talker."

"He is very self-confident and can have a commanding presence," Maggie said.

Maggie became quite sick during her first pregnancy and was prescribed medication that they later learned could cause birth defects.

"When Jessica was born, the first thing Glen did was count all her fingers and toes," Maggie recollected. "He told me that she was okay."

"Raising the baby was a joy to both of us, and I loved being a dad," Glen said. "But I did not want to have another until we could get Jessica trained and out of diapers."

"Jessica was three when we had Lisa," Maggie said.

"We believe strongly that God has a plan for us—marriage, kids, a home to raise them. Our kids were taught to respect the Lord. We both worked, had careers," Glen said. "We made sure that our children learned our faith and that it was a part of their lives. We went to church each Sunday without fail. We set goals for ourselves, and both of us worked hard to make them happen. For one, we were able to save enough money and bought this beautiful home on the river."

The couple became grandparents after Jessica got married.

"Being grandparents is amazing," Maggie said. "Lisa was a teacher by that time. She loved being around her two nephews."

"We were concerned about Lisa's relationship with Tom from early on. He just seemed 'off' to us, if you know what I mean. Just not right. He would tell us and tell others that Lisa was crazy, she was unstable. None of that was true," Glen said. "They broke up a bunch of times, but when she found out that she was pregnant, she went to Tom and told him, and they got back together."

"I told her that she would be a fine single mother. She was an award-winning teacher, she loved kids, and being a mother would just come naturally to her. But she went back to him anyway," Maggie said. "We last saw her at a local football game. We were with Jessica and the grandkids. Lisa was starting to show, and she was glowing. She looked beautiful."

"We invited her to come with us to the river house that weekend. She told us that Tom had something planned for them so she could not make it," Glen continued. "A few days passed, and Lisa did not show up for school on Monday. That was not at all like her. She never missed a day. We went to her apartment and her dog was there alone. I know Lisa would have not left that dog by herself."

"For nine days, the police were searching for her," Maggie said.

"I told them that she must have been kidnapped and tied up somewhere. I could not imagine her not being alive," Glen said.

Lisa's body was found buried in the middle of a field not too far from her home. She and her unborn baby had been shot and murdered.

"The police believed that Tom killed her, and they asked us to help get him charged," Maggie said.

"We went on TV with the police and the state's attorney, and Tom was with us. He was crying before the press conference; I told him that he could do it, and he did. He got up in front of that microphone asking for help in finding Lisa. Somehow, we held it together, knowing he had killed her," Glen recounted.

Tom was arrested and charged with Lisa's murder. He never made it to trial.

"He killed himself before the trial was scheduled to start," Maggie explained.

"When we were planning her funeral," Glen said, "the pastor told us that we had a choice—that we could either be angry at God or try to see the positive—that Lisa and her son were in heaven and with God, that they were at peace."

"I really believe that God does not give you more than you can handle," Maggie affirmed. "We held tightly to that and to our beliefs. Glen needed me to be strong, and I did my best."

"The first few years after she died, we both just threw ourselves into our work. I lobbied the state legislature and worked to have a law passed that would view the murder of a pregnant woman as a killing of two people—the mother and her unborn child," Glen said.

"I went back to work. I asked people not to treat me differently. I wanted things to be as normal as possible. Being at work made me feel better," Maggie said. "After my dad died, my mother came to live with us. For some reason, that was the straw that broke the camel's back."

"Maggie was angry a lot and very bitter. We went our separate ways to do our own thing and did not talk much," Glen said.

"I was stressed and starting to feel bitter about what had happened to Lisa and our grandchild," Maggie said.

One night, Maggie left their bedroom and slept in the guest room.

"We committed a long time ago that we would always sleep together. I said to her she was always angry at me and it did not seem she even liked me anymore. I asked her if she wanted a divorce," Glen disclosed.

"I did not want a divorce. I was just crying so much all the time, and I did not want to keep him awake," Maggie clarified. "I needed some help to deal with the grief. It was like it had been stored up and came rushing out all at once."

Maggie went to counseling to help her with the grief and sadness.

"It is always there, I think I will be sad, and it won't go away," Maggie revealed. "But we went through it all together and we are closer again."

"We both believe in a higher power, that things happen for a reason," Glen stated.

Glen makes regular visits to the field where Lisa and the grandson he never knew were murdered. Two white crosses stand alone.

"I can't do it. I just can't go," Maggie said. "I give him bulbs to plant flowers."

"It is beautiful there. It gives me solace, and I feel close to her. I say the Lord's Prayer, and I know Lisa is with me," Glen said.

OUR TAKE

The first things that come to both of our minds are the same: faith, strength, and courage. On the other end of the spectrum? Tragedy. Grief.

Glen and Maggie had a path, they made their plans and their goals and built their lives around all of that planning. They knew that they wanted to have children, save their money, and buy a home. The couple also came together and decided to save for a second home, a place where their children and grandchildren would visit for years to come. Above all, Maggie and Glen's common faith and belief in a higher power was at the heart of their lives together. They planned their work and their life goals. Then God stepped in, gave them something that they did not— and really could not—plan for and over which they did not have control, their daughter's murder.

"This was a horrible, horrible thing. I am not sure there is anything worse. Lisa's death was also the first real bump in the road, the first major deviation from their plan," Julie emphasized. "Things went off script, so to speak. That in and of itself pressured and stressed their relationship."

The two dealt with the loss very differently. Glen threw himself into a project, dedicating himself to getting changes in homicide law passed. Maggie went right back to work. And she did not want to be treated any differently—even though she was certainly aware that the community knew what had happened, since this was a major local news story, she still wanted to be treated the same as before by her coworkers. "Being at work helped her; it made her feel more normal," Julie reasoned. "But it did not give her time to grieve," David asserted. "It seems to me that she went through the motions up until the point after her father had died when her mom came to live with them. That was when she started to spiral."

Elizabeth Kubler-Ross was a psychiatrist who developed a model called the Five Stages of Grief. The stages are denial, anger, bargaining, depression, and acceptance." Her model was first applied to people who generally had been diagnosed with an illness. In another book that was published after her death, she expanded her model to cover all kinds of personal loss, including the death of a loved one. "I do understand the theory—and this is a lawyer talking, I know, not a psychiatrist—but I question why everyone who experiences loss must go through each of those stages," David said.

"You are not the only one," Julie said. "There actually is a fair amount of criticism of the Kubler-Ross model.

Many researchers have argued that people need not experience all the Kubler-Ross stages at all, much less in order." It was almost as if Maggie tried to jump right to the "acceptance" stage, throwing herself into work, wanting for everyone at work to treat her the same as before her daughter's death. But when she slipped into the "anger" stage, she and Glen began experiencing trouble in their relationship.

In *US*, a more recent book written by Terrence Real, the author talks about the need for couples to experience harmony, disharmony, and repair. A relationship is not just all happy flowers and sunshine. In other words, a couple needs to experience gray skies, conflict, and bumps in the road. The relationship is actually strengthened by experiencing harmony, confronting disharmony, and ultimately working together to repair whatever harm may have occurred in the experience of that disharmony.

"So what I am saying here is that while they experienced this awful tragedy, it was not until a few years later that the disharmony came to the surface via Maggie's anger, seemingly directed toward Glen," Julie clarified. "The two had to confront Maggie's anger. That anger gave rise to disharmony in the relationship."

And experiencing the disharmony and facing it helped them repair things. It all seems connected. Years after Lisa's death, Maggie's grief bubbled up, resulting in conflict that led to the couple working together to move forward. It took a good while though. As anyone who has experienced it knows, grief is not on a timeline.

And we also see through these folks that there are multiple ways to grieve, to experience and deal with grief. Glen faces it by going to the place where Lisa was killed, finding some connection to her in that field. "In large part, that comes from his faith that everything happens for a reason, that there is a plan for us," Julie explained. "His belief in a higher power, his faith that there is a reason for the tragedy, that really is what Glen holds onto. It makes him feel better and brings him some peace of mind."

Bulitt Point Takeaways

- Grief has no timeline
- Don't bury trauma, confront it
- Disharmony can strengthen a relationship

CHAPTER 3

Rebuilding Trust After a Financial Collapse

"He lost my mother's house."

Those were the first words Lindsey uttered; no hello, no introduction, no small talk.

Paul is not heavy, but not really in shape either, and the couch creaks a bit when he sits next to Lindsey. His faded blue button-down shirt is untucked and slightly pilled around the collar. Paul sighs. He knows the story.

Lindsey is clearly ready to talk. Her black hair is pulled back in what Julie likes to call a "summer do." In black slacks and a white blouse, she looks dressed for a job interview.

"I grew up in this great house not too far from here with my brother, my sister, and my parents," Lindsey began. "When Dad died, my brother and sister had already moved away and I was the only kid nearby. A year or so later, Mom got sick and needed regular care. But since the house was paid for, she didn't have many expenses. The money she had let her afford in-home care."

Paul interrupted. "Not 24/7 around the clock though. I went over most every day. Cut the grass, fixed stuff, odd jobs. Made her meals now and again."

When she died, Lindsey's mother left the house to her. "My brother and sister were not upset at all," she said. "They felt it was fair for us to have it since I had cared for Mom for so long."

The couple moved into Lindsey's childhood home with their two daughters, then twelve and fourteen. A carpenter by trade, Paul had no shortage of projects at the new house.

"Paul went right to work. He finished the basement so the kids could have a place to hang out and built a front porch. He did a great job," Lindsey remembered.

"Don't forget all those closets," Paul clarified. "I think half the house was closets and racks. I remember spending hours measuring and cutting those racks, with the right number of shelves for shoes and clothes plus others up higher for longer dresses."

"Teenage girls, you know," Lindsey added.

They both laughed.

For most of his career and while his kids were growing up, Paul worked for a local contractor. "It was mid-size projects mostly, cabinetry for new kitchens or bathrooms, decks, porches, refinishing basements, and rehabbing houses for investors looking to flip properties and make some money," he recalled. "It was a good job, regular work and pretty good pay. I never worried that we would not have enough work to do."

When their kids finished school, Paul decided he wanted to start a small home contracting company and work for himself. Lindsey was supportive of Paul venturing out on his own. "School was paid for, and he had worked so hard for that company. It was something he wanted, and I wanted it for him. We were both excited."

Unfortunately, Paul's new business did not succeed as he expected. "We took a home equity loan against the house to invest in the business," Paul went on. "Equipment, a couple of employees, and three trucks. With all the contacts I had made over twenty years or so, I had no reason to think we would not do as well as I had done working for someone else. When things didn't pick up, I had to draw more on the line of credit."

After a year, Paul had gone through all of the home equity line—all without Lindsey knowing he had done so.

"We set it up so it only needed one signature to borrow more, and the money just went right from the credit line into our bank account," Paul explained.

Lindsey jumped in. "He didn't tell me that the business was having problems, so when I saw the deposits going into our account, I just assumed he had gotten paid on a job."

Paul never told Lindsey a thing. Once the line of credit was tapped out, he went and got credit cards, on two occasions even signing Lindsey's name to the application and using another address for billing. Paul kept the situation under wraps and did not discuss any of the troubles with Lindsey.

"Look," Paul stressed, "it was my job to take care of my family, like my dad did and his father did before him. I did not want Lindsey to worry. Plus I felt like I could get us out of it. All I needed was time and some more money."

Another five months passed with debts continuing to mount.

Creditors were calling Paul and sending him dunning notices. "If there had been any other way out, I probably would never have told her," he conceded. "The only way was to sell the house. So I told her. Asked her to sit down in the kitchen, just laid it out: the debt, the repossessed trucks, everything."

Lindsey's response was predictable. "I was upset. I was always behind him. I supported him right from the beginning. I had no idea he was lying, robbing Peter to pay Paul and all that. All he had to do was tell me. Fill me in. Maybe I could have helped," she pointed out. "Instead, he lied to me about the business, he lied to me about the debt, and then just dumped it all on me all at once. I think I was in shock, not processing or whatever the term is. After a few minutes of staring into space or wherever, I was just like, 'Hell, there is no way we are going to pay for all of this.' Then it hit me, right there at my mom's table, in my mom's kitchen. There *was* one way. I had to sell her house. Of course, Paul already knew that."

For the next few days, Lindsey did not speak to Paul. "He thought I would be disappointed in him if he told me what was going on."

Paul interrupted. "Oh, come on. We've been through this. Of course you would have been disappointed."

Lindsey did not miss a beat. "We'll never know now, though, will we? We went into that thing together. We were a team. Supposed to be anyway. I just did not want to talk to him. I couldn't."

"It didn't go on forever, thankfully," Paul continued. "We had been together a long time. I knew what she felt. I knew what she was thinking. The house she grew up in, the house she loved—it was lost because of me. I was actually kind of glad that there was not a big blow-up, screaming match kind of thing."

"That's the thing," Lindsey responded. "I was not thinking that at all. Sure, I was pissed. And yes, I would be lying if I didn't tell you that it crossed my mind that this idiot cost me my mom's house. What he didn't understand and maybe still does not completely get is that it wasn't the house. It was the lie—the lies. Not telling me what was going on. That is what really caused me to question things, whether this was someone I could trust—even after all this time."

Ultimately, the house was sold and the couple moved into a rental a few miles away.

"That apartment might as well have just had a sign on the front door that said 'LOSER,'" Paul remembered. "That's how I felt every time I walked in there."

For some time, Lindsey did not do anything to ease that guilt. "I didn't want to let him off the hook. I know that sounds bad. But here I was, living in a one-bedroom apartment that was about the size of my daughter's room in her sorority house. I knew he felt awful, but it took me a long while to be able to do what I knew I should, to tell him it was okay, that we would get through it."

The couple never went to counseling.

"Neither of us wanted to talk about it, I don't think," Paul revealed; "for different reasons."

Did they just have an epiphany and decide they loved each other and the relationship was more important than this one situation?

"No, not at all," Lindsey replied. "It took a lot of time; a lot of time apart, not doing the things that we were used to doing together. Dinners out, movies at home, walks in the park—we just skipped a lot of that for a long while."

"We hung in there, I guess you could say," Paul said. "Slowly we started to laugh more, the tension began to fade."

"I know that other people might have talked things through, maybe in counseling. But that just was not me," Lindsey acknowledged. "I was mad. I was disappointed and hurt. Talking to someone about it was not going to make it better."

"She needed time. I understood that so I did not press anything.," Paul added. "I worked, did things around the house, tried to talk about anything that might make her smile or laugh. Anything but losing that house."

"Things are better now, sure," Lindsey concluded. "Will we ever get back to where we were? I don't know, to be honest. I just don't know. But at least we showed up. We are still together and here talking to you."

OUR TAKE

Why is it so difficult to be transparent and truthful with our husbands, our wives, our partners? Many times, it's avoidance and shame. Lying is sometimes seen as a third natural reflex, if you will; a defense mechanism to cope with threats. "You have heard of fight and flight, right? Lying is also a natural reaction for some people in times of distress. People lie because it is easier not to talk about what they did or didn't do," Julie reasoned.

People also lie to protect themselves and preserve their self-esteem. Here, Paul was upset with himself, he was failing. Every month he kept tapping into that credit line was another reminder of his failure. He was embarrassed, yes, but his lying to Lindsey was not malicious.

"Paul had a good career, and he was supporting his family. And he was clear about it—it was his job to raise his family. So he starts his own business, down the tubes it goes, and with it Lindsey's mom's house," David explained. "So he lies and he covers up. And what does that do? It makes everything worse. Paul's business doesn't get better, the family finances get worse, and his relationship with Lindsey starts to crumble."

Isn't it a bit more complicated, though? Should Paul shoulder all of the blame? Lindsey is a smart woman. She clearly put her head in the sand and ignored the signs of financial troubles. She mentioned that she looked at bank statements and was aware of money going into the account. Why did she not see the money going out? "Something does not fit for me," David commented.

We all have a part in or some responsibility for most circumstances we find ourselves in. Lindsey found it easier to not be involved in their finances, and that was a choice she made. It then became easier for Paul to continue to deceive her. They are a team, and she should have asked or taken more interest in what was happening. Blaming someone else is not fair when you didn't do your share.

"It's that old evil serpent again—the failure to communicate," Julie concluded. "Lindsey should have kept on top of things, asked him how business was. Do you really think he would have directly lied to her face? I don't." Paul's dishonesty was certainly under the surface—what I don't tell her won't hurt her. It was not until he had no wiggle room—no other option—that he finally spilled the beans.

At the same time, there is a depth to Paul's dishonesty. Failing in business is not a crime. But when Paul hid it from Lindsey and continued to do so, that was just devastating—not only to their financial lives, but to their relationship as well. "He almost lost more than money," Julie emphasized.

"In lawyer speak," David imparted, "Lindsey's blind eye made her an accessory. Say there was a bank robbery. Paul robbed the bank, but he needed a ride to get there. He gets in the back seat of a car that Lindsey is driving. Paul has a mask on his face and a gun in his hand. Lindsey does not really pay attention to who gets in the back seat, what he has in his hand, or what he is wearing, and she drives him to the bank to commit the robbery. She has culpability. Same thing here."

Most certainly Paul should have been up front from the start. Had he done so, Lindsey would have been in the loop. Maybe she could have helped, or they might have closed the business before falling further in debt.

"Even if the business still failed, at least they would have been in it together," Julie said.

"It is so important for couples to talk about finances early on," David said. "What do we have, what do we owe, where do we want to go, what do we want to save, what is okay to spend and what is not?"

"And do what the two of us learned the hard way—what we should have done from the beginning," Julie said. "Set goals for paying off debt, for saving...that sort of thing."

And be honest. Don't hide financial problems hoping they will magically go away. They won't. Just ask Lindsay and Paul.

Bulitt Point Takeaways

- Know and discuss your financial circumstances
- Being embarrassed is preferable to being dishonest
- Financial failure does not necessarily equate to relationship failure

CHAPTER 4

Staying Connected After a Child's Death

Barbara and Steve have been married for fifty-one years. Retired and living nicely in a small East Coast beach town, the two of them have three grown children and ten grandchildren.

"We spend a fortune just on birthday presents," Steve told us. "Had to give up on all the holidays, though. We'd go broke."

Barbara rolls her dark brown eyes. "What he doesn't know won't hurt him," she said.

Barbara grew up in an upper-middle-class section of Boston. "We had what we wanted," she described, "but both my parents worked for it. No one gave us anything. There was no inheritance to live off of like some of the girls I knew growing up. Both my sister and I understood that to make it in the world, you had to work hard."

"Hard" comes out as "hahd" in her Boston accent.

Steve is also from Boston. "The other side of those tracks though," he clarifies. Both his parents immigrated from Eastern Europe, and Steve, an only child, grew up in a small apartment. Steve's father was a barber who walked to work each morning, his mother a seamstress. "Growing up, it didn't bother me being an only child since I had a lot of cousins that were like brothers and sisters to me. When I got older, though, I felt I had missed something and knew I wanted children," he recalled.

The couple met on a blind date, having been fixed up by Steve's friend and Barbara's cousin who themselves were dating since both of them thought the two would be a good match. Although Barbara was seeing someone else at the time, her cousin was so adamant she had to meet Steve that she agreed to go. After less than six months dating, all while Barbara was still seeing the other man, Steve told her he loved her and asked her to marry him. She waited a day before accepting Steve's proposal. "At that point, I thought it was time to let the other fellow know," Barbara explained.

They were married for two years before having their first child. "It was wonderful, being a father—all that I expected," Steve said.

Barbara got pregnant again less than two years after Sarah was born. The baby was due around the same time as Barbara's younger sister's wedding. Barbara's obstetrician was also planning a vacation around the due date. The obstetrician suggested that Barbara have labor induced prior to full term to be sure she would not miss the wedding.

"Looking back all these years later, I do not believe that he thought too much about my sister's wedding," Barbara said. "Those were the days before big medical practices that had several doctors who could fill in.

He did not want to chance missing his vacation," she asserted.

Although Barbara's labor and delivery went fine, it was just a few hours after the birth that the doctors told Steve and Barbara that the baby's lungs were underdeveloped and she was in distress. Three days later, the baby died.

"Her name was Anne. After my grandmother," Steve said quietly, blinking and looking away.

Steve and Barbara reach for each other's hand.

"It was devastating, it really was," Barbara revealed. "I remember my friend coming to visit me in the hospital. She brought beautiful purple flowers—my favorite color—and a baby gift. She didn't know. I had to tell her that our baby died. My friend was so sad. I felt bad for her."

Both Barbara and Steve agree that the death of their child was the most difficult thing the two of them have had to endure as a married couple.

"I didn't know what to say or how to comfort her. So I didn't say much of anything," Steve admitted.

Long before therapy and grief counseling became more accepted and their benefits understood, many couples would have turned to friends or family for support. But that was not their way. Stoic to the core, Barbara states in a very straightforward and matter-of-fact fashion, "I didn't need anyone to say or do anything. I did not need to spend any time talking about it."

There was no funeral for Ann; no photos, no memorial service.

"You just didn't talk about those things," Barbara remembers.

The hospital took care of all the arrangements, including the burial in a local cemetery for infants. They both know where it is, but even now, all these decades later, neither of them has been to Anne's grave site.

"We decided to put it behind us and that was that," Steve said. "I was raised by tough, hard people. My mother and father were both immigrants. I was taught that life is hard and bad things can happen, but you can't wallow in it. So we didn't."

Two weeks later, the couple attended Barbara's sister's wedding.

"We danced when we had to. With the rest of the family," Barbara said.

"Otherwise we just sat. Sat and held hands. Just trying to survive and move on," Steve concurred. Barbara and Steve managed to do both.

"It was very painful. Very sad," Steve affirmed. "But losing the baby was our loss—the two of us. Sharing everything with friends and family, talking about it all—that was just not our way. Still isn't."

"You do what you have to," Barbara added.

They had two more children, a boy and a girl.

Over the years, Barbara and Steve would mention Anne now and again.

"Not too often," Steve acknowledged. "We did sometimes talk about having our son Robert after Anne died, how thankful we were for him and that we may not have had him had Anne lived."

"They call them 'rainbow babies,'" Barbara explains, "a child that is born after a sibling passes."

Barbara and Steve went on to have a fourth child, Jennifer, two years after Robert.

"They are all wonderful children. They have careers, spouses, and families of their own. We could not be happier," Barbara declares.

"I remember when Jennifer found out about the baby," Steve said. "She was about twelve when she learned that she had a sister that died at birth."

"Oh, God. She was furious," Barbara went on; "mad at us that we did not tell her. I am sure that many people may think it was terrible, not to tell a child that she had a sibling. I am not sure there is a right or wrong. But this way was right for us."

"Listen," Steve stated firmly, "we tried to explain to her that as a couple, we had to put the whole thing— all that happened—in a box. We sat her down, we did, and tried to help her understand that is just how we handled it. We were sorry she was upset, but we did what we thought was right." He paused. "And that's it."

"She was so angry at us. I know other parents may have told her, but at the time it just didn't seem to be the right thing. It was a sister she would never know," Barbara reasoned. "And we didn't want to go back."

"We didn't want to talk about it, even then," Steve emphasized.

"I know it is different now. People talk about everything," Barbara conceded. "Someone dies and you see it on Facebook the next day. I don't know. Maybe that is better. Maybe not."

"We may have grown up differently," Steve said, "but we both got the same strength from our parents. We just both seemed to understand that we were in it together, needed to protect and support each other."

"Even in silence," Barbara said.

OUR TAKE

Julie struggled with this interview. "I was very concerned with how they handled the baby's death when it came to their other children," she disclosed.

"People were different then. Times were different," David interjected.

"I get that," Julie responded. "But not to tell her—I don't mean to be judgmental, but their daughter was going to find out eventually. They should have told her, long before she was twelve."

Is she right, though? Even now, isn't it reasonable for a parent to keep something like that from a child? It seems that it should be a parent's prerogative to raise their child in the best way they see fit—excluding abuse and neglect. After all, as parents we are vested with the responsibility of protecting our children. How we do that varies from one person to the next. There are many truths that parents keep from children, like Santa Claus and the Easter Bunny.

"Yes, but not to tell a teenage daughter that she had a sister that died—when both her siblings and other people do know—I think that was a mistake," Julie pointed out.

Jennifer was certainly angry when she found out. And rightfully so—everyone else in the family knew about the baby except her.

"And her parents were unapologetic about it. I could have predicted her reaction," Julie continued.

"It was a little surprising that Barbara and Steve did not seem to expect that type of reaction from her. And when they spoke with her, it was almost like a science class—very matter-of-fact, not much emotion. Just, like, 'This is what happened, this is why we did not tell you, and that's that.' You know what I mean?"

"These are stoic people," Julie concluded. "Their way of handling it was just that—their way."

And what to make of Barbara's mention that she and Steve "suffered in silence"?

"I am not a big believer in silence being golden," David noted, "but again, it seemed to work for them."

Compartmentalization is a defense mechanism that is often used to get through hard experiences, situations that involve intense emotions.

"It's the 'putting it in a box' strategy of handling something. Barbara and Steve were adept at that," Julie said. "It did come at a cost when Jennifer found out about it. Family secrets have a way of growing through the years like snowballs, and when people find out, it can be devastating. Their daughter may have wondered what else they didn't tell her."

In terms of Barbara and Steve, it's as if their avoidance of emotional expression and suffering in silence also kept them from grieving.

"Grieving is important. It's a process. It takes hard work and requires a lot of energy. The sadness does not go away, but it fades as time goes by and allows someone to remember the good times they had with the person that they lost," Julie explained. "As a therapist, I can't help but wonder if it would have been easier for them if they had shared it with others. Sometimes the load feels lighter when you share with others, even other couples who lost babies, just to know they weren't alone."

Barbara and Steve never got to enjoy any time with that baby. She was born and she was gone.

"And it seems to me that this is where their strength and togetherness as a couple carried them through," Julie went on. "Barbara and Steve could have easily grieved in their own way and drifted apart. But they didn't. They both supported each other. They pulled themselves up, went to that wedding, and then looked forward and raised three other children. They supported each other—in their own way—maybe not with words or as much communication as I would have liked to have seen from a therapist's perspective, but they truly were—and are—a team."

"I have been involved in a few cases where the parties lost a child. They became more and more distant from each other both emotionally and physically," David recalled. "Oftentimes, what I have heard in those cases was that the deceased child had been what really kept the parents connected and together. When the child died, they could not find—or maybe did not want to find—something to replace that loss in terms of maintaining their connection."

Statistics tell us that there not a more traumatic event than losing a child. Close to 80 percent of couples who lose a child end up divorcing. There is plenty of research out there that shows that parents may start to develop negative feelings about each other, begin to fight more, or withdraw from the relationship. Some blame their spouse for what happened and start to feel anger or resentment for one reason or another.

"Not Barbara and Steve, though," David stressed. "These are not people to wear their hearts on their sleeves. They had a certain toughness individually that is conveyed by the endurance of their relationship. The loss brought them even closer together, and may have served as more of a bond."

"That is the other side of the continuum," Julie added. "There are parents who sustain that loss and are able to pull together, share their loss, grieve together in their own way, and figure out how to move forward. These two took enormous joy from their other children, and that helped them put their daughter's death behind them and in that box."

Both Barbara and Steve inherently just knew that they did not need to have a lot of discussion about it. Not a lot of talking. Just doing.

Bulitt Point Takeaways

- Compartmentalizing can help to get through difficult circumstances
- Avoid blaming your partner
- Successful communication can include nonverbal communication

CHAPTER 5

Assembling an Adoptive Family

John and Jennifer are both on their second marriages. A native of Harrisburg, Pennsylvania, John is the oldest of four siblings. "Coming from a big family," John remembers, "I knew I wanted that too."

Although they tried for a couple of years, his first wife was unable to conceive. "Not having babies was always hanging over us. She felt that she was a failure," John explained. "Ultimately, our marriage failed too. Not only because we were unable to get pregnant, although that certainly added to things. Neither of us was really happy."

John and his first wife divorced after thirteen years.

Jennifer grew up in Prince Georges County, Maryland, a suburb of Washington, DC. She was also raised in a large family, with two brothers and two sisters. Jennifer was only nineteen the first time she married. "I should have known it would never work," she acknowledged. "All the signs were there: his drinking, the cheating. But we had fun together, partying a lot with no real responsibilities. I thought the bad stuff would go away if we got married. He asked me, so I said yes."

Not surprisingly, marriage did not eliminate "the bad stuff." Her husband's drinking got worse and his late nights out of the house more frequent. "He never admitted to it, but I knew he was running around on me," Jennifer recalled.

After about eight months together, Jennifer packed up and moved back home with her family.

John was thirty-eight and Jennifer thirty-two when they first met at a sports bar near Jennifer's home. John was a mid-level manager for the US Census Bureau and Jennifer a paralegal working for a lawyer near the county courthouse.

"She caught my eye right away," John said. "I can still tell you exactly what she was wearing that night."

Jennifer noticed John also, but even after more than ten years, still felt the pain of her first marriage failure.

"I had no intention of getting into any real relationship," Jennifer points out. "I mean sure, I dated, but for the most part stayed away from men after the divorce—to be honest, I was pretty comfortable with my life. I had a good job, was saving money, and with maybe another year, would have had enough to move out of my parents' house and find my own place."

Despite her misgivings, Jennifer gave John her phone number. "He seemed smart, sure of himself. Those biceps didn't hurt either," she affirms, giving John's arm a squeeze.

John kept at her, calling and emailing. They went on a few dates, then a few more. Both fell in love and were married a year later.

"It was something we talked about early on," John noted. "We both wanted children, so we started trying pretty much right after we got married."

After two years of trying, they were still unable to conceive.

"Having been through this before," John revealed, "you can bet I was worried about the whole 'not being able to have kids' thing wrecking this marriage. I wasn't going to let it happen."

"He was unbelievably sweet, so good to me during that time," Jennifer said.

John regularly reassured her that they were in it together and would find a way to have children.

"One way or the other," John declared.

They spent a year working with an infertility specialist, attempting three IVF treatments, but with no success.

"I just didn't see light at the end of that tunnel, aside from the light of bankruptcy," John ruefully admitted.

They spent more than $30,000 working with the infertility doctor before deciding to try the adoption route.

"I knew that stress could have an effect on fertility," Jennifer articulated. "I read a lot about men who had trouble with sexual dysfunction that was caused by the pressure of having to conceive. Add on to that a sprinkling of financial stress and it's easy to understand all the pressure that John was feeling."

"I went into the work with the fertility specialist thinking it would be great. Sex all the time, and even more when she was ovulating," John interjects. "I mean, how bad could that be?"

For both of them, however, it didn't live up to the billing. "We both felt like we were on a timer, that sex was more of a responsibility—another chore that had to get done during the day," Jennifer clarified.

"I felt like the panda at the zoo that gets yanked in every so often to try to get the female pregnant," John agreed. "It got to the point that I would have rather been eating bananas or whatever it is pandas eat—anything other than having sex. And the cost of those injections started to get to me. I started calculating how much each failed treatment cost us. The pressure just kept rising."

"I'm not sure what he is complaining about," she went on. "I was the one who had to lay there for five minutes, legs propped up and hoping that this time it worked. I was miserable. Not just because I wanted to be pregnant, but also because I was sick of the whole process. The shots were not much fun either."

Despite the two of them feeling stressed and put upon by trying to have a baby, John and Jennifer were able to keep it together.

"We tried to laugh about it as much as possible," Jennifer affirms. "We even came up with a contest to see how long it would take for him to finish."

"For a while, my record was about a minute and a half," John disclosed. "Then it started taking a long time. I know she was getting impatient, but I just could not do it."

"It was just awful. Sometimes it went on for what was like forever," Jennifer concurred.

The stress bled into other aspects of their lives as well. Jennifer had trouble sleeping. John started to experience some severe back pain.

"She was not sleeping, and I was in pain and uncomfortable all of the time. Plus I felt like a failure," John revealed.

"We both were irritable and unhappy," adds Jennifer.

Jennifer helped herself by exercising in the mornings before work and spending time meeting for coffee and talking to a couple of close girlfriends on non-Saturday mornings.

"It wasn't commiserating since those girls were both married and had kids, but they let me get it out and complain about things. Just talking with someone other than John was helpful; therapeutic even," she expressed.

John handled things differently. "I didn't really want to talk about it," John clarified. "I didn't think any of my buddies was going to feel sorry for a guy who was being forced to have sex a lot. Every time I thought about all the money we were spending, it just put me in a really bad mood. I thought that I was better off trying to ignore it."

Jennifer became worried about John keeping it all inside and the pressure getting to be too much for him. She suggested they go to couples counseling. John initially refused but agreed to go after they started the adoption process.

"I did some asking around and found a group of other couples who were going through much of the same things as us," Jennifer recalled. "It was really helpful for John to see that there were other men who felt the same way he did."

John agreed. "I was surprised. Never having been in any kind of therapy before, just hearing other husbands talk about this stuff was good for me," he conceded. "Looking back, I do think that had a lot to do with it, but when we were in the middle of all that regular monthly failure, we—me—I just could not figure a way out."

"So we looked at another way of making a family," Jennifer continued. "This was not like my first marriage when we were unable to conceive. I was younger then, in an unhealthy and unhappy relationship. I didn't have the patience then. Not to mention I really was not sure that the two of us should even have kids."

"With Jennifer it was so different. We knew where we were in life and that we wanted to have a family together," John reiterated. "We looked at agencies, the possibility of fostering first also. Ultimately, we found a lawyer who specialized in representing parents through the independent adoption process. I liked that idea because we were participating more in the process, rather than waiting for an agency to call."

"Working with the lawyer felt like we had more input and control over the process," Jennifer commented. "Unfortunately, neither of our families were particularly supportive of adopting a baby. John's parents are old school. They just could not get their hands around the fact that they might have a grandchild that was not really their 'grandchild.' "

"It was a difficult discussion for sure," John confirmed. "To be fair, coming from a family with four kids and raised when we were, there was not much in terms of experience with adoptive families. You know, it was the whole 'but they are not going to be your blood' thing."

"My parents thought we were being impatient and should keep trying," Jennifer described. "My mother was worried that I would not feel the same about an adopted child. I never had that worry. Neither did John."

The adoption route was a success. John and Jennifer had a boy. A year later, they went back to the same lawyer, and after a few months of searching, found another biological mother and adopted a second child—this time a baby girl. John Jr. is now at the University of Maryland studying engineering.

"No such luck with Kate, though. That one wanted to get away. She is a sophomore at San Diego State University. She wants to be a psychologist," John explained.

"A bird's got to fly," Jennifer added.

"I'm not sure the bird had to fly across the country," John interjected, "but she is happy there, and that makes us happy."

Both Jennifer and John enjoyed the adoption process.

"I liked reading the letters and information sheets about possible biological mothers—what they were looking for in adoptive parents," Jennifer shared.

"It became a bonding activity for us. We would sit on the couch with some wine and read the stuff together. It was fun," John went on.

"Deciding to adopt got us back to who we were as a couple," Jennifer declared. "We laughed more, I slept more—thank God."

"Looking back," John remembered, "some of it was luck, some of it was work. We were lucky in that we were such a good fit for each other. We did our best to avoid confrontation, we did not have those terrible arguments that other couples had. Sure, we had our share of dirty looks and walking the other way, but generally we both knew when to try to talk to the other or when to give the other some space."

"Flexibility and patience, those were the keys," Jennifer concurred.

Words to live by.

OUR TAKE

A lot of this couple's story sounded familiar to us, from the frustration over not being able to conceive to John thinking he was going into a month-long sex orgy—"Until he realized it was not what it was cracked up to be," as David said. Also, like the two of us when we were trying to get pregnant, Jennifer and John really did not accept failure. Trying "the old-fashioned way," as we like to say, was not working. A lot of people would have gotten sullen, depressed, or angry. Probably they would've quit. These people did completely the opposite. They pivoted, turned to adoption, and raised two great kids.

"One piece that grabbed me here was that they both had unhappy first marriages. It is clear that those experiences helped them push through and make a family together," Julie points out. "This is really more your area though. Do you think the fact that they both experienced failures motivated them to stick together at all?"

The truth is that second marriages statistically have a significantly higher divorce rate. Where the overall divorce rate in the United States hovers around 50 percent, it is over 60 percent for second marriages.

"Many of my clients over the years have been in second marriages that failed," David noted. "I think people usually are a bit older and more set in their ways, and it is harder to be flexible with a new partner. The most frequent areas of conflict in a relationship are family, money, and intimacy. Add to that what I call a 'general malaise,' and there are your areas that send couples careening toward a divorce."

Those high conflict areas are even harder to avoid in a subsequent marriage. One spouse may have their own money, or alternatively, problems with money. One may have children from the first marriage, along with support obligations to the former spouse for alimony or child support. There is also the possibility that one spouse has developed certain sexual interests or desires that may or may not match up with the new spouse. Finally, one spouse may have an ex to deal with in terms of conflicts around their children, such as visitation, medical issues, or academic problems.

"There is this concept called 'second wives syndrome,'" David commented. "It's a bit of a misnomer; should really be called 'second spouse syndrome.' The second spouse's gender is irrelevant. That person can be in a position to have to deal with an angry or vindictive first spouse, and they may have to live with ongoing conflict that their spouse has with spouse #1. And again, those conflicts are usually about money or children."

So why even get married a second time?

"People don't want to be alone, right?"

"With John and Jennifer, this former spouse issue did not exist," Julie clarified. "This couple dug in. They both had the desire and ability to work together and be on the same page on a number of issues, including adoption. You remember how it was for us. Some people were supportive, while others could not understand how we would want to raise children that were not biologically connected to us. I really hated that 'our blood' thing. It never mattered to me how we got a baby. The baby was ours, and that was all that mattered. The fact is that I have a lot in common with each of our kids. It made no difference how we got them."

Both John and Jennifer had tough first marriages. Hers was an abusive relationship with a spouse who obviously could not or did not take the relationship seriously in an adult way. For him, it was all party and play.

"Possibly an alcoholic," Julie surmised.

"My sense of John's first marriage was that it was simply a mistake. He was never really happy as far as I could tell," David observed. "When it came to their not being able to have kids, there may have been some disappointment, but the feeling I got was that John was more relieved than anything else. He knew that the relationship was not a good one."

Both of these people certainly learned and grew from the experience of their prior failed marriages. When they got together, both were committed to success.

"These two communicated regularly from the beginning. They agreed to try the infertility treatments, and both worked at it for a good while. Then when each realized the other was getting frustrated, they continued that line of communication and decided to try adoption," Julie noted.

The truth is that not all of us are fortunate enough to just exist on the same page with our long-term partner and have the same jumping-off point. Most of us have to work at it. This is not to minimize the effort that both John and Jennifer put into staying connected and together. For the rest of us, it may not come as naturally, but we can all use the same tools. Talk to each other, do it regularly, and be a team in your approach to adversity.

Bulitt Point Takeaways

- Laugh and use humor to navigate a challenge
- Maintain friendships outside your relationship
- Give each other space

CHAPTER 6

Navigating Adultery and Illness

Kimberly was diagnosed with Parkinson's Disease ten years ago, a few months after her fiftieth birthday. "At first, I just thought I was getting older. There were some quirky things," she recalls. "My hands would tremble a bit, not all the time, but enough to notice. I was stiff a lot—my neck, my back."

"I noticed she was having issues with balance," Ben added. "I didn't think too much about it until she fell."

The couple had some friends over on a Saturday night for some dinner and drinks. Not one to drink much, Kimberly had a glass of wine.

"And she did not even finish it," Ben remembered; "a couple of sips at most. That small amount should not cause much in terms of impairment even for Kim."

On her way up the stairs, Kimberly screamed and fell back and down. "Thankfully, I'd only made it up a couple of steps," she explained. "I just felt kind of a whoosh of dizziness; I held myself still, but down I went."

A trip to her family physician led to a referral to a neurologist, and tests and more tests.

"Ultimately, I got the Parkinson's diagnosis. I was scared to death, but kind of relieved at the same time.

We caught it early, so that was good. And at least I knew what it was," Kimberly described.

Kimberly's lifestyle took a major hit. Pretty, blonde, and green-eyed, Kimberly had been an athlete in college and up until the diagnosis was an avid tennis player and self-proclaimed gym rat.

"I really had a great life. I was in good shape, got myself toned up, and felt great. Most people thought I was ten years younger," she pointed out.

"And those eyes," Ben piped up. "Just killer gorgeous. Still are."

"Maybe a little dimmer these days," Kimberly demurred, gazing away.

In the year following the diagnosis, Kimberly's condition worsened, and she started experiencing a lot of what she called "the Parkinson's crap."

"It was awful, these horrific nightmares: bugs crawling on the walls, mice in my bed, ants all over me," she revealed.

Often when waking up in cold sweats, Kimberly found herself alone in bed.

"I was often anxiety ridden and too amped up to go back to sleep. I missed Ben not being there, but it was okay," Kim shared. "He was doing the best he could with everything. At home, he picked up the slack. He took care of the grocery shopping each week, the pharmacy for my meds, and whatever the kids needed and of course driving them everywhere. He needed to work, so no, I was not upset or even questioning why he was not home some nights."

"I started staying out later once every couple of weeks, then it became more frequent. At first, I would just stay late at the office, even if I could have gone home and worked from there," Ben admits. "After a while, I started meeting coworkers for diner, staying for drinks, watching a game. The other thing just sort of happened."

"Just sort of happened," Kimberly repeated.

"I did miss having sex with Kim," Ben stressed. "For a long time, it was great. Some people complain that sex loses its luster as you age or with kids in your life. Not with us. It was regular, sometimes not as frequent. But fun and an important part of our relationship—at least to me."

"He's right. Our sex life, at least in my mind, was good. Frequent, different, and fun. We were not that couple who only had sex on special occasions or just on Saturday night. And we didn't just do it in the bedroom. We had sex in the kitchen, even in the car," Kim laughed.

Ben smiled. "Got a bad leg cramp once," he said.

Another symptom of Kim's disease was a loss of sexual interest.

"I really had no sex drive at all. It just was not something that interested me, and I had enough to think about. It never crossed my mind that he would ever look around and sleep with someone else," she observed.

"Anyway—and this is nothing I have not told Kim at this point," Ben acknowledged, looking at his wife, "the late nights turned into business trips that I was asked, but not required, to make. My coworker went too; we met up at bars and restaurants and ended up in the hotel together."

"It was deceitful," Kim asserts.

"Sure, sure it was. But at the time I really did not think it mattered. I was getting a need met—and that was it—there was no real emotional attachment, no commitment," Ben responded. "I came home, did my work around the house, took Kim to medical appointments. We went to dinner, the movies. Whenever she felt up to it, I mean."

The two discussed getting some counseling to talk about things and ultimately decided to meet with the same pastor who had married them twenty years earlier.

"When we went to couples therapy after it all came out, that was the part that was truly surprising to me," Kimberly articulated; "that Ben really believed that somehow his having sex with another woman didn't matter. I mean, really? It didn't matter? Just too much."

"I was definitely living a lie, and I felt bad about it," Ben concedes. "But again, Kimberly had no interest, she was focused on her health, and I didn't think—and I know this sounds s***ty—but it wasn't fair. Sure, you both are going to tell me how selfish I was thinking, 'Poor Ben, his wife doesn't want to have sex because she has Parkinson's disease,' but I felt how I felt. I mean, yes, Kim was sick, but that didn't mean I no longer had a sex drive," he said.

"Maybe it should have," Kimberly commented. "I knew things were different, and maybe the thought of his having an affair crossed my mind. But it was fleeting. I just did not think that was possible."

"It took some time before I even noticed or thought anything was unusual," Kimberly recounted. "The late nights at the office were not terribly out of the ordinary. He had gone through periods with the company before that when he had to stay late. The travel was a little strange, for sure. But more than that, he seemed a little disconnected—going through the motions kind of. He is right. He did do stuff at the house and take me out, he was attentive, but there was something missing, and I could not quite figure it out."

Kimberly ultimately confronted him.

"It just kind of came out, half joking even. I asked if he was having an affair. It was over coffee one morning, newspaper on the table. Just a normal morning."

"By then," Ben remembers, "I was done with the lying. I wanted to come clean and get it off my chest. I knew it would hurt her, but in that moment, I thought it was best to tell her what was going on."

Julie asked what he said to Kim.

"I put my coffee down, told her I loved her and was sorry. I told her that I was sleeping with this woman from work and that it didn't mean anything," Ben described. "Just physical. I had no feelings for her. I loved Kim and wanted our marriage to stick."

"Sure, I was hurt. I walked to the bay window in the kitchen and cried. I felt deceived, lied to. Hell, I *was* deceived and lied to. But the truth is that I wasn't really crying about Ben cheating on me. I was crying because I felt it was my fault. If I hadn't gotten sick, it never would have happened," she reasoned.

"I asked her if she wanted me to leave," Ben recalled. "And she did. So I left that afternoon. Packed enough clothes for a week or so, my computer, work stuff. We sat the kids down and told them that I was moving out for a while. We didn't say whether it was permanent, just that we needed some time to ourselves. Of course, the kids knew something was up. The dynamic in the house was not the same. We did not argue in front of them, but we were cool, we didn't speak much. There was certainly tension, and they could feel it. So I left and moved into one of those extended stay hotels."

Over the next three months while they were separated, Ben was back at the house every day, sometimes for hours on end. He took Kimberly to her medical appointments, got her groceries, and made many of her meals. They went together to their pastor for marriage counseling.

"He was doing everything he had always done. It's just that he did not sleep at the house," Kimberly clarifies. "And he promised that his relationship with the woman was over."

"I did make that promise. Many times. During our counseling sessions and when it was just the two of us. And I kept it," Ben said.

"I love him, and I know he loves me," Kimberly affirms. "It certainly was not a high point in our relationship, but at the heart of things, neither one of us wanted to lose the other. Of all that came out during those sessions, that was what really struck me to my core. We both wanted to stay together."

"There was a lot of grief in those sessions. I felt guilty. He felt guilty. We both felt miserable," Kim shared.

"But we felt miserable together," Ben laughed. "Seriously, I think that was important to me anyway. Knowing that Kim felt bad, even though none of this was her fault. She just felt bad about how her illness made me feel—and act."

"We talked a lot about the dishonesty, the damage it did to our relationship. The loss of trust. Sex as well," Kim reflected.

After close to a year, Ben moved back into the house.

"It was not a 'same as usual' kind of thing. We could not go back," Ben acknowledged.

"That's right, for sure," Kim agreed. "He understood it was not 'forgive and forget' for me. It was 'forgive,' though. And move forward—that too."

"We are happy again. I think so. I know that the affair won't go away, but I hope that Kim understands that it was a moment—one that I am sorry for— and that what we have together is so much more," Ben offered.

"I have learned a lot since then," Kimberly noted. "It does creep into my mind, but not often; not nearly as often as it used to. I push it aside and try to think of something else—our kids, our next trip, anything positive."

"Life dealt us a few things that no one expects or even thinks about," Ben said. "But we're still standing."

OUR TAKE

There was a lot for this couple to manage and work their way through, including Kimberly's illness, the affair, and the separation and subsequent reconciliation. But let's start with the reason that Ben strayed.

"He said he was getting a need met. Those were his words," David points out. "He needed to have sex, Kimberly was unable to, and so he found someone who could fill that piece of his life for him. I'm not saying it was right, but it seems like a logical explanation to me. You think it was more than that?"

"You ever heard of masturbation? Never mind, don't answer that," Julie replied. "Come on, it was not the sex. It's like you have said many times before, we all want to be noticed, appreciated, paid attention to."

Ben wanted someone to pay attention to him, take care of him, show him some affection. Ben was taking care of Kimberly: getting her medications, making her meals, and doing the laundry and whatever else she and the family needed. "Carpools, sports, activities—all of that," David continued. "He also had to work to keep his family above water financially. It's a lot of responsibility, and her illness was a big change to his life also. Everything focused on her or on the kids. No one was asking how he was doing or feeling. So he sought out companionship, someone who smiled at him, noticed him, and complimented him. And had sex with him."

What if he had been able to keep it to himself and not tell Kimberly? Ben said none of it mattered.

He loved Kimberly, and he said that the affair was a diversion, something to keep gas in his tank. "If she never knew and the relationship he was having helped him manage his new reality, one could certainly argue that it might not have mattered to their relationship. On the other hand, though, Ben felt guilty, and he just was not able to keep living with the guilt, holding it in and keeping it to himself." Julie observed. "'No harm, no foul' was his thinking."

Except there was harm. Ben's conscience was harmed. The guilt he felt was harmful. And then there was a foul. A lot of them. His relationship with Kimberly was permanently damaged, at least to some extent. His family, his relationship with his kids, it all changed. "So yes, there was harm and plenty of fouls," Julie concluded.

There have been several studies of relationships where one partner admits to cheating; more than half of them broke up almost immediately, while another 30 percent stayed together for a while but then broke up later. Only 15 percent of those couples were able to recover from infidelity and stay together.

"In couples that I have seen over the years, infidelity is almost always a relationship killer—one way or the other. Sometimes people don't really get over it but still stay together," Julie explained. "Couples stay together for the kids, and to keep their family intact and under the same roof. There could also be financial reasons to stay together. I wonder how many of that 15 percent that stayed together were really happy afterwards. At best—and this is with even the most forgiving of partners—there just has to be some damage, some loss of trust."

"I have seen a lot of cheating in thirty-six years of doing divorce work. In my experience, without sounding gender specific or even sexist, women are more apt to forgive infidelity than men," David stated. "In heterosexual relationships, I have found that men often cannot get over their wives having sex with another man. Often, they get angry—very angry. The divorce process can be even more difficult when one spouse has cheated and the other is angry."

"Hell hath no fury like a woman scorned" is a familiar proverb adapted from a line in the 1697 play *The Mourning Bride* by William Congreve.

"I have actually found it to be the opposite— Hell hath no fury like a *man* scorned. I think that is probably because men tend to be more territorial, while women are usually more realistic."

"I agree. A man often feels more violated— someone took his wife, invaded his space, took what was his," Julie concurred. "Women, I think, understand that sometimes even the best of husbands thinks with his penis, and as a result, these women can look at it more like a mistake, that he didn't really mean anything or something along those lines, and deserves to be forgiven. I am not saying it is so for everyone, but there is some logic there."

"But I think Kimberly was in a tough spot," David added. "Here she is trying to manage her own reality of living the rest of her life with this illness, and to a great extent relying on the support of her husband, when she discovers he is sleeping with someone else."

Will Ben cheat again? Might his guilt, the harm he caused to Kimberly and their relationship, serve as a deterrent? And what about Kimberly?

"I think she is trying," Julie offered. "Kimberly is focusing on all the good that Ben has done for her and the kids—all the extra effort, the work, everything. There is a lot of good there."

Fear is another emotion bubbling somewhere below the surface—Kimberly's fear of navigating her illness by herself. "That has to be running through her head," David asserted. "Ben does a lot for her, and not out of duty so much I don't think as out of love."

Regardless of the why, there is still the fact that they both are sticking with it. Ben does not want to leave. He loves Kimberly and wants to stay together. They both obviously lean in a little on their faith, and that is what pushed them toward the pastoral counseling.

"Religion brings a lot of hope and strength to a lot of people. Many pastors have extensive training in counseling couples. The training is obviously somewhat different from the education I got, and it has the faith component built in," Julie elucidated. "All of us who work with couples, whether secular or not, usually have the same framework in mind. I call it 'relationship repair.' This couple worked together to try to patch and repair their relationship. They took advantage of outside supports that really helped them work through a lot if issues and hurt. Also, they really love each other. That much is clear."

But will it last?

Bulitt Point Takeaways

- We don't have to forget to forgive
- Let your partner know if you feel ignored
- Every relationship needs repair at some point

CHAPTER 7

Building an Unconventional Family

Reece's father died the morning we met.

"My dad was sick. He was eighty-four and had chronic heart problems for much of his life," Reece told us. "He and my mother were married for fifty-four years. My father was a fireman. He lived the life he wanted to. We were probably in the lower-middle class, but we never wanted for anything."

One of four kids, Reece was raised in the Midwest. "With Midwest values," as he said.

"I learned values on my own," his partner Rob added.

When he was twenty-one, Reece told his parents that he was gay. His father was a career firefighter and devoted to his faith.

"He would not accept it," Reece recounted. "I remember going to church with my parents one Sunday morning. My uncle was the minister there. His sermon was all about the need to uphold Christian values and how to live a good Christian life. He went on about how it was our responsibility to fight for Christ and against others who did not live a 'good Christian lifestyle.' I felt attacked, really. I got up and walked out and did not talk to my parents for a long time."

Reece moved to the East Coast. "I wanted to see what life was like outside where I grew up," he explains.

After his move, Reece's parents came to visit and saw him perform at a church service.

"My dad told me that he was never so proud of me as when I took that stand against him and mom," Reece remembers. "They came around to my being gay; not happy, but accepting."

Rob grew up quite differently. "I was raised in the foster care system. When I termed out—and by that, I mean turned eighteen—my foster parents told me that I had to leave. They were no longer getting money from the state. I was an adult, so I had to get out."

Rob lived on the street.

"All my belongings—everything I had in the world—were stuffed into a garbage bag," Rob shared.

With unmatched grit and determination, Rob forged his own path. He went to college and became a successful banker. Money and finances, however, were not to be his life's work.

"Reece and I founded Comfort Cases, a nonprofit organization to help kids experiencing foster care," Rob said. "Comfort Cases sends backpacks to kids—all over the US and now overseas as well—filled with necessities; a toothbrush, toothpaste, soap, and shampoo, that sort of thing. Every backpack includes pajamas, a book, a journal—and a stuffy, too."

"He likes stuffed animals," Reece chimed in.

"I don't want any kid to have to live their life out of a garbage bag," Rob asserted.

"We met at a bar—the Green Lantern in DC," Reece recalled. "There was definitely an instant spark, that connection kind of thing."

"We started dating, tried to take things slow," Rob said.

"Not that slow," replied Reese. "On our first date he asked if I wanted to have kids."

"I wanted to be a dad. That was the key for me," Rob points out. "I definitely felt something for Reece from the start, but if he didn't want a family then I did not want to take things further."

Rob's desire to be a father grew out of his foster care experience.

"My foster mother cried when I told her that I was gay. She told me that she was sad for me because I would never have kids. I knew that I wanted kids, but I also wanted to prove her wrong."

"It took me aback a little bit. I mean, we were on our first date," Reece admitted. "I had not given it a lot of thought, but I knew that I liked children and enjoyed working with them when I ran a local children's church program."

Together now for eighteen years, the couple has five adopted children, all of whom came to the family through the foster care system.

"Once we got the okay from the state to foster, we got four of the five in less than six months," Rob noted. "All the kids are different, and all of them are special in their own way. Like with a lot of foster and adopted kids, though, there are special challenges."

"It's not just the ethnicity," Reece stresses. "Our family is multiracial for sure, but all our children have come from varying backgrounds, some with connections to a biological family, some not. Some had been in multiple foster homes and went to any number of schools before becoming part of our family."

"I have a special place for all of them," Rob affirmed warmly. "Have I told you about Alex? I am so proud of him."

The couple adopted Alex when he was seventeen and close to aging out of the foster care system.

"I was speaking at a local school, and Alex came up after, asking me if I would sign his copy of my book," Rob remembered. "He reminded me so much of myself, I just had to find a way for us to adopt him. He went from foster care to living on a farm. We all hit the lottery with Alex. Just an amazing boy."

Moving from being foster parents to becoming adoptive parents was not all that easy.

"We are two gay white men. That was the first issue. We wanted to adopt children of color, another hurdle. There were many doors to open," Reece articulated.

"We went through all the hoops, and we were persistent," Rob said.

"We kept fighting—with social workers, case managers, judges. But ultimately, we were able to adopt our kids and build our family."

"Obviously our lifestyle changed, and that really made a big difference in our relationship. We went from this neat and well-kept home, weekend dinners out, and staying late at parties, to puffed cereal all over the house," Reece went on.

"Nice china to paper plates and clothes just everywhere. I like things neat and in order. Having kids changed all that," Rob acknowledged.

"The adoptions were stressful and easily could have taken a toll on our relationship," Reece observes. "But we never drifted apart, and I can't remember too many times when we got off the same page."

"We no longer had all the time together that we had before the kids. But we both have faith and are totally committed to each other. Basically we held tight to each other and our faith in God and just rode the waves together," Rob concurred.

"It's interesting, I know," Reece reflects. "After the experience with my parents all those years ago, I could have left the church, feeling as if I did not belong there because of who I am. But that is not what happened. I knew that God had a plan for me and that my uncle was just wrong. I belong in the church just as I am."

"We both have a very deep faith. When we got together, we researched and found a church that would be a home for us and our family. Church is a place where we can go to get away from all the outside noise and feel close," Rob expressed. "And that was really important in all we have done as a couple to build this family. From fostering to adopting and raising kids with multiple health and behavioral issues, we really needed to have some slice of life to ourselves."

"We are very different in a lot of ways, but I think we complement each other," Reece said.

"I'm loud, forceful, and opinionated. I'm all about me, really, I am," Rob concedes. "Did you know I changed his name?"

Although Rob's partner was born and raised under the name "Maurice," Rob was not comfortable with the name and shortened it to Reece.

"It stuck. Some people still call me Maurice, but Rob and many of our friends call me Reece," he clarifies.

"Reece is quiet, not at all outspoken. He is about family, he always puts himself after me and the kids," Rob shared. "Reece can just look at me from across the room, and I can tell if I said or did something that was out of line. But whatever that might be, he waits until we are alone to talk about it. Nothing in front of others."

Rob and Reece have developed very clear roles in the family.

"I don't think we would still be together if Reece had not given up his career," Rob stressed.

"Rob's job could support our family. So my job was to take care of the family and the house, be more hands-on from day to day with the kids," Reece explains. "If there was a problem at school or one of the kids needed to get to the doctor, I handled it."

The couple has recently sustained a painful loss.

"Two of the kids left. Our daughter decided that she should live with her biological family," Rob disclosed. "So she sits in a little apartment babysitting, basically doing nothing."

"One of the boys got in legal trouble. He calls us names, says we aren't his parents," Reece continued. "It's so hard. Losing those kids, but knowing they are still there."

"It really pisses me off, to be honest," Rob interjects. "How ungrateful can you be?"

"Rob feels hurt—rejected," Reece revealed. "I understand that, but we need to let them find their path, whatever that is. Hopefully, both will reach out and come back to us in some way. But if they don't, we will have to live with it and move on. We gave them a life and a chance, and at this point I don't know that there is anything else we can do except be there when they call."

"If they call," Rob replied. "In hindsight, I can't say that I would do it all again, I really can't, if I knew then what I know now, all the heartache that I would put Reece through. It's been a lot of struggles." He shakes his head and looks at the ceiling. "A lot of pain."

"That's interesting," Reece commented. "In many ways, maybe I agree. Lots of what has happened with the kids has hurt us. It has for sure; after all we have given and done for them, to just walk away as if it was nothing. It's a very deep hurt. But at the same time, I enjoyed raising the kids. It was very fulfilling for me."

"It was like for much of our time together we have not even been a couple. Going from one issue to the next without a break has been exhausting much of the time," Rob reflected.

"Maybe so," Reece responded, "but we have made a point of staying connected. We spend time together at night, when everyone is asleep and things are quiet."

"It does not matter how long or difficult the day has been," Rob confirmed. "We get in bed and put on the TV. Sometimes we talk a bit, often we watch a show together. And it's a show we both like and won't watch without the other. Just us together."

"It's a simple thing but those few minutes at night—just us—it keeps us grounded, reminds us that we are in all of this together, that we are a team."

OUR TAKE

We were worried about the timing of this interview. With Reece's father having just passed, we did not know what to expect or how it would impact our discussion. There was no real plan to go down that road, but we could not have a discussion without talking about his dad.

This is a couple who came from quite different backgrounds. You have Reece, a Midwestern boy with "Midwestern values," as he put it. He grew up in a home that leaned in hard on family and on faith. It certainly was not perfect, as we heard, but he had a solid core, a consistent family unit growing up.

"Not entirely supportive as we heard, but well rooted and secure," David noted. "Except for his sexuality, it sounds to me like Reece's family was supportive. And even with that, they came around. I loved the story about his father telling Reece how proud he was when he stood up for himself; how meaningful that was, particularly maybe with his dad just passing. That really touched me. Rob, on the other hand, had no such support or consistency growing up," David said.

Except for the consistency in living a life filled with insecurity. And what should we make of that "my mission was to have children" thinking that Rob had?

"This is a reflection of Rob's determination, his strength," Julie affirmed. "He clearly knew—even early on—that he was meant to have a family, raise children. I think his foster mother certainly served as additional motivation for him, but it was more of an icing on the cake kind of thing. Ironically though, it is Reece who has handled the lion's share of child-rearing responsibilities."

"You could say that Rob accomplished that mission, he got what he wanted, but left the heavy lifting aspects of parenting to Reece," David points out. "Rob is not shy—he is a strong personality. I mean, come on—he just decided that he was not crazy about the name 'Maurice' and started calling his partner Reece. Rob essentially changed his name."

"The real point isn't that Rob changed his partner's name—it's that Reece was fine with all of it. He was fine being called Reece, he was unselfish when he gave up his career, and he was obviously comfortable taking on more of a traditional at-home parent role," Julie reasoned. "That is what worked for them. If Reece was not accepting or had not been as malleable, they would have had real trouble staying together. Rob said as much himself."

Rob and Reece's division of responsibilities is however not that much different than many families where one parent is the primary wage earner and the other's job is to manage the family and the household.

Given their backgrounds, it is not at all unusual that Reece is the "stay at home" parent, so to speak, while Rob is the family's primary wage earner. Reece had the benefit of growing up with parents who cared for him, who loved him. He had the benefit of role models in both his mother and father. Rob had none of that.

"I think, though, that Rob recognized he missed out in terms of seeing what good parenting looks like," David said. "He knew that Reece had more of an understanding of what it takes to be a parent on a day-to-day basis and has taken that in and learned from it. Rob also developed a close relationship with Reece's father."

Faith is important to both of these individuals, another link in their relationship chain: "deep faith" as Rob put it. Their faith, however, was developed from different places and over varying paths.

"It's my 'equifinality' concept," Julie says, "They arrived at the same destination from varying starting points. Reece was raised with faith; it was basically built into his DNA as a child. Rob seemed to find it on his own. Although Reece left his parents' church, he found another when he came to the East Coast. Then the two of them researched and chose a church together."

"When you look at these people, it really is two pieces that fit—Rob's outgoing, strong personality, Reece's quiet strength." David added.

It took us both back a bit when we learned that Rob and Reece now have second thoughts about fostering and adopting their children.

"I do think that the timing of our talk had something to do with that reticence and those second thoughts coming up for them," David asserts. "Two of their children left recently."

"They most certainly are in the midst of experiencing feelings that are the result of ambiguous loss," Julie offers. "Dealing with two holes in their family—the kids are gone, but they are not gone."

Rob is clearly angry about it. Both of them are hurt. Of course they are. It is not all that different from what the two of us have experienced with our daughter. She has been gone from our lives for over a decade, but she is still out there—somewhere. It is still there, but the years have lessened the pain, the anger, and the hurt. Rob and Reece have not had the same benefit of time to mask some of the pain.

"The fact that they fit so well together and understand each other's roles, strengths, and weaknesses, that is what has held Rob and Reece together—that and their faith," David concluded. "I love that they watch TV together each night when things quiet down."

Whatever it takes to keep that closeness is all that matters. When a couple makes it through difficult things like these two have, their relationship strengthens. They develop and share intimacy in a way that is natural and comfortable for both of them.

"At church or in front of the TV late at night—it does not matter—those are the glue moments," Julie concurred; "the moments that keep them bonded and together."

Bulitt Point Takeaways

- Make time for just the two of you, even if it's just for a few minutes each day
- Discuss each partner's roles when building a family
- Shared faith can be a source of a couple's strength

CHAPTER 8

Outlasting a Child's Cancer

Linda and Joe are both fifty years old. Married for twenty-eight years, they were born and raised in the Boston area and have lived there all their lives. The youngest of three children, Linda is the only one of her siblings to marry and have children. She grew up in a mildly observant Jewish home.

"We observed the high holidays and some others, and we lit candles on Sabbath, but were not regulars at synagogue. I had a Bat Mitzvah, but almost no one showed up because it was in the middle of a snowstorm," she remembers.

Joe was raised in an Orthodox Jewish family where there was strict compliance with the earliest tenets of Judaism.

"We kept strictly kosher in the house and everywhere: prayers and reading the Torah every day, and when we went to synagogue, men and women were separated," Joe said.

Joe has two siblings, a brother and a sister, both of whom are now married with children of their own. His parents both died more than twenty years ago, but not before instilling a strong core of traditional Jewish beliefs and customs in all of the children.

"All of us are Orthodox, and we have passed what we learned and discovered in our own childhoods on to our children. It's basic and central to who we are and who we want our children to be," Joe averred.

To be closer with Joe and his values, Linda decided that she would become more practiced in traditional Judaism. She went for the ritual baths (called a "Mikveh") at a nearby synagogue and studied many of the Orthodox core values and traditions.

"Gosh, I read more prayers than I ever thought existed," Linda recalls.

"Linda knew that I wanted her to at least be familiar with things, but I did not force her in any way," Joe noted. "Like everything else she does, it was her decision. She decided, and that was that."

Soon after the wedding, Linda and Joe bought a 1950's era home in the same suburban Jewish community where Joe grew up. Much of what Linda learned during her Orthodox training stayed with her but was not practiced with any consistency.

"I did some, sure. I told Joe that I was 'Modern Orthodox,'" she elucidated.

Unlike other Orthodox women who lived in the neighborhood, Linda wanted to have a career outside the home. She went to school and learned to cook.

"I was not quite a chef, but close," she explains. "I went to lots of family homes, both in and outside of our neighborhood. I cooked Sunday night dinners for some families, made food for funerals and births, and did parties even. You name it, I cooked all kids of foods, not just kosher meals. I could do a Greek meal,

Italian, even Chinese. Kind of an Orthodox Rachael Ray," she laughed.

The couple had two boys, Andrew and David, within three years.

"We went from a quiet house to a full house real quick," Joe commented.

Being a full-time mother was fulfilling, but Linda wanted more.

"When the boys were both old enough for school, I decided that I wanted to get my real estate license."

Almost twenty years later, Linda still works with a local real estate firm, helping both buyers and sellers in the residential market. Each of the boys started going to an all-boys summer camp when they were eight years old.

"It's a beautiful place up in the mountains with a lake and trails, and lots of swimming, sports, and other activities. It was hard for them at first, being away from home, but they both loved camp and looked forward to going each year," Joe recalled.

"And we looked forward to the few weeks to ourselves," Linda added.

David was ten when he went to spend his third summer at camp. "We got a call from the camp nurse that he was complaining of a backache and was having a hard time with some of the activities," Linda recounted.

"Knowing he could be a little dramatic, we talked to David and told him that maybe it was the bed that was hurting his back and that his counselor was going to give him a different mattress. We encouraged him to tough it out and told him that he would be okay," Joe continued.

Less than a week later, the nurse called again. This time she said that David was still complaining and the doctor who visited the camp each week had taken a look at David and wanted to talk to them. The doctor called an hour or two after they spoke with the camp nurse. He told them that David had a lump on his back and need to leave camp for an evaluation right away.

"He suggested that it might be nothing, but it was unusual. He told us that we should have it looked at right away and not wait until David's camp session ended," David remembered.

They went to the camp and picked David up that evening. Two days later, David was diagnosed with Hodgkin's Lymphoma.

"The oncologist told us it was a 'bad news-good news' type of thing, which really irritated me," Linda revealed. "He told us that David would need probably two years of chemotherapy and intensive treatment for the disease but that the survival rate for kids was very high—ninety percent or something like that."

Joe immediately shared the difficult news with friends and family.

"Within like a day, the whole neighborhood knew about David," Linda stressed. "We were getting meals and calls, offers to help with Andrew, just about anything. And that really upset me, that Joe would just go and tell everyone without discussing it with me. I mean, it was a family situation, not all the neighbors' business. Everyone did not need to know."

"I really could not understand the problem, to tell you the truth," Joe admits. "I grew up in this community, and that's what we did. We shared our successes and our failures. Everyone knew what was going on, and everyone wanted to help. What was wrong with that?"

"I understood the community where we lived. People were concerned, sure, but there were also a lot of busybodies. Plus, Joe didn't talk to me first before he started sharing it all with the neighbors," Linda clarified.

"They were not just our neighbors," Joe asserted. "They were our friends."

For the next two years, David went through regular and often painful treatment for the disease.

"He lost a lot of weight, lost his hair. He was sick a lot of the time, and we had to be very careful about his diet," Joe recounts. "When he wasn't tired or too weak to go out and ride his bike or play ball—anything to just be a kid—we were both always worried that something was going to happen to him."

During his treatment, Linda and Joe spent so much time taking care of David, there was not much time to focus on anything else. Gone were the nights together talking about each other's day and the hour or so after the kids went to bed to catch up on a TV show.

"We were both tired and running on empty a lot of the time. We had one goal: to keep David alive, to do whatever we could to keep him alive," Linda stated.

"We shared the work, every responsibility, every clean-up after he was sick, the travel and waiting for him to get treatment at the hospital, staying up with him at night. Anything that needed to be done for David, we did it equally," Joe went on.

"I know it was hard on my husband, trying to balance everything with David, while trying to keep on track at work and still be a good father to Andrew. It was a tough time for all of us," Linda discloses. "What happened though, now that I think about it, is that we just stopped being a couple, two people who were in love and who cared for each other. Instead, we almost were coworkers at the same job with the same boss, doing what we needed to do until we were exhausted, then going to sleep for a little bit before getting up and doing it all over again."

"Through it all, we stayed in love, though, I can tell you that. I always felt the love was still there," Joe reflected. "We were both scared, sure. But fear can be a wellspring for love."

Although their love for each other did not wilt, the intimate part of their relationship did.

"I think we may have had sex twice or maybe three times at most in a year or year and a half," Joe noted. "She was not interested, and to be honest, I wasn't either."

"It was not just the lack of sex," Linda articulated. "There was really no intimacy of any kind. We had love for each other, like Joe said, but we did not express it. There was no holding hands, no hugs, no communication between us offering support. We lived together. We worked and we both had a job to do to get our son better. There was no time to take care of anything else except our kids."

Despite Linda's misgivings, the community continued to support the family. Joe's boss gave him more flexible hours; the private school that the boys attended waived tuition for both of them.

"I was relieved that we were not getting in trouble financially," Linda recalls. "I also came to be thankful for all the help that we were given."

"I think she started to accept the support for what it was—support—and not people wanting to snoop in our private business and gossip about how David was doing, or that we were not getting along," Joe observed. "It took me awhile, but I did begin to understand that bringing friends and family into our home and into our situation was maybe not the best thing to do for Linda, at least not without letting her know that I was sharing and commiserating with some friends."

As David started to show improvement, the couple went together and spoke with the local rabbi.

"I thought we should see a real professional, not the rabbi. But at that point, our relationship was pretty strained, so I went along with it," Linda continued. "You would think that all we had been through and done together in the time that David was really sick would have made us closer. Instead, it was totally the opposite. We became less connected, like I said, less of a couple and more like partners working on a project."

"I was glad she went. I did feel like it was a compromise on Linda's part, you know, going to our rabbi in this community that I brought her to live and raise our children in rather than to a therapist or marriage counselor," Joe acknowledged.

"I tried to go in with an open mind, and to be honest, it did help even though I was not comforted or helped by the faith-based overlay of our sessions," Linda shared. "The rabbi did convince us to go on an overnight retreat with other parents who had kids who were sick. I was opposed at first. It seemed as if it would be too painful. It was hard, but sharing stories with the other couples somehow made us more connected. I'm not sure how, but it did."

"Even now, all these years later, we still go and talk to the rabbi, even if there is nothing particular that we want to talk about or work on," Joe said. "We both realized that our relationship was on the edge, and after all we had been through, we needed to try."

"I think about it a lot," Linda added; "David being sick, how we started to drift apart and forget about each other. I'm thankful we made the effort to appreciate everything—and each other."

OUR TAKE

These two were very different in how they processed the news of their son getting sick. Joe leaned on his community, right? He shared the news with his friends and family. Linda would have preferred more of a "this should be kept in our family" kind of thing.

"Some people, like Joe, are external processors," Julie explains. "They want to share their news and talk to people about it. Linda was more of an internal processor. She wanted to keep the situation more private. When individuals in a relationship process things differently, it can cause conflict. Linda was not happy with Joe's sharing of David's illness, but it did not rise to a really significant conflict between them. In other couples you might see some serious disagreement."

This is similar to our relationship. Julie tends to want to talk to people about issues that we might be facing or things we are doing. David prefers to keep things more between us.

"You do. And I generally have tried to respect that as I know how strongly you feel about us keeping certain things private," Julie affirmed.

"I definitely see where Linda was coming from here—on both fronts. She felt that David's illness was not for public consumption. She also understood Joe's need to share and get support from others," David offered.

There was another common issue that David's illness caused them to face. These are great people who went through what is unimaginable for many of us. It caused them to alter their path together. The focus of their relationship had to change.

"A couple's 'relationship focus' is something I work on with couples," Julie related. "Certainly goals can be part of a couple's focus, as well as expectations. Say a couple gets married and plans on having several children, but because of a health issue, they can't have kids. Some couples may change their focus to fostering or adoption, while others might just decide not to have children and their focus can move to traveling more or a new career."

"With Linda and Joe, the focus of their relationship—their goals—raising their kids, being part of a community, Joe advancing at his job—that all went out the window," David observed. "Their sole focus and only goal was to get their son healthy."

What happens when a couple's focus changes and their goals are altered? Conflict arises. It's not unlike what we experienced when we decided to adopt. The two of us became laser focused on finding a baby. We ran ads in Penny Saver papers all over the country—in Indiana, Texas, and West Virginia, to name a few. We put in a separate phone line for those women to call. Sometimes Julie would talk with a caller for hours only to never hear from the person again. The entire process was so time-consuming.

"It was not the only thing we talked about, but it certainly took up a lot of our time together," David noted.

"That's my point," Julie stated. "We were so homed in on accomplishing that goal that we often did not take the time to talk about other stuff, relax more, or do other things together. The change in our focus put a strain on our relationship. And with Joe and Linda, it was the same thing—a change in relationship focus—but brought on by something entirely different, their son's illness. That is exactly what Linda said—that she and Joe were not really communicating, they were not connecting except when it came to David and taking care of him.

"The unintended consequence of this hyper focus," David said, "was that the direct relationship between the couple got pushed to the rear. The 'them' had no purpose other than to take care of their son."

As a result, Linda and Joe neglected the rest of their relationship. The intimacy between them—the rest of their lives really—took a back seat and faded away. It was not a purposeful thing. It just happened. Once their son got better, they both realized what they had done to the relationship and worked to rekindle not what was lost exactly, but what was missing."

"And let's not lose sight of the part that their religious beliefs played in helping the two of them. Although Linda was not thrilled about seeing the rabbi, she went because she saw it as a way to bring the two of them back together."

"It sounded to me more like they both recognized the need for some help. I mean, come on, look what they went through with their son. It's hard to imagine. It took every ounce of strength each of them had to get through it," David reasoned. "I think Linda would have preferred someone like you or another professional, but she understood the importance of Judaism in Joe's life. So she agreed to meet with the rabbi. Being Jewish meant something to both of them—Linda too. Maybe it was more vital to Joe than Linda, but she went, and with an open mind despite her reservations. They went together."

"And it helped," Julie concluded. "Often parents who have sick children suffer irreparable damage to their relationship. Blame, guilt, anger, and other emotions can just get in the way and block their ability to stay together and move forward."

With so much focus and so much energy being dedicated to their child, it is not surprising that taking care of their own relationship dropped off the radar. "Stress levels rise, and by their very nature, the stresses are magnified. These two were not just worrying about David, there also was worry about Joe's job and making sure their other child was managing okay, as well as visits to the hospital and the costs of prescriptions. So much more," Julie reflected.

"There was no way that their focus could not undergo change. But they stuck together, spent the time—'made the effort' I think is how Linda put it," David pointed out. And it was no small effort. Their lives changed; their relationship changed. The two of them needed to put the work in to avoid coming apart.

And they did.

Bulitt Point Takeaways

- Intimacy can come in many forms
- Maintain your relationship focus
- Couples therapy is a tool to relationship success, not a last resort

CHAPTER 9

Establishing Family Boundaries

Pam's father died a month after she started high school. An only child who'd always been close with her mom, the bond grew even stronger after her dad died and continued when Pam went to college.

"I played two sports in high school, field hockey and lacrosse. My mom was at every game, every practice. She was always there with me," Pam remembered. "Some of the other girls laughed at me a little—about my mother always being around—but I think some of them were jealous. They had parents who were too busy to make it, who couldn't help with carpools or team parties. A lot of them were on their phones even when they did show up. Not my mom."

When Pam went to college, she chose a school close to home.

"I was planning to live at school, on campus, and my mother said that was what she wanted me to do," Pam continued. "I was sure she really did not want me to go, though. And I felt bad, knowing she would be alone at home. So I lived at home for the full four years. There were some times that I thought I was missing out—I didn't get the experience of living in a dorm, I skipped I don't know how many parties. I almost joined a sorority, but it seemed like a big-time commitment, and I would be away from home a lot. Plus I would have had to live in the sorority house. I could not do that to my mom, move out."

Pam and Ryan met when they were college seniors, both in the school's business department.

"It was at a sorority party—kind of like you two," Ryan interjects, holding up his copy of *The Five Core Conversations for Couples*.

They hit it off right away, began dating, and got engaged just months after graduation.

"I was not all that close with my parents, so Pam's relationship with Ginny was very cool to me—unique, I mean. Not like anything I ever really had with my mom and dad," Ryan noted.

After graduation, both got jobs in the area. Ryan was renting an apartment, Pam living at home with her mother.

"We were seeing each other most every day after work and getting together on the weekends. Ryan was paying some exorbitant amount for rent, and one night while we were all watching a movie, Mom suggested he move into our house and live in the basement rent-free," Pam recalls.

Ryan jumped at the offer and moved into Ginny's basement, where he lived for the next two years until he and Pam got married. "I liked the idea of him being downstairs, and I think Mom was happy to have a man back in the house," Pam went on.

Staying with Pam's mother allowed them both to save money and buy a home about twenty minutes away from Ginny's house just before they got married.

A few months after the wedding, Ginny asked the couple to her house for dinner. She told them that she wanted to sell the house.

"Basically, my mom felt that she could not take care of it anymore. She wanted to travel and didn't want the hassle of maintaining and worrying about the house," Pam explains. "I was a little surprised. She had never mentioned selling before. I was sad but understood. It was where I grew up, where Ryan and I'd had some great times the last couple of years. But it did make sense, and I told her she should do whatever she wanted."

What came next, however, took both Pam and Ryan off guard.

"Ginny asked if she could just 'have a room' at our house," Ryan revealed. "She wanted a place to stay when she was in town and was expecting a nice windfall from the sale of her house, with prices having jumped so much during the pandemic."

"Again, Mom said she would not be around much and planned to rent an apartment in Florida for most of the winter. She just wanted to be able to visit, and to spend time with grandkids when they came," Pam elucidated.

"We did not even give it a second thought," Ryan acknowledges. "She gave me a place to live that let me be close to Pam. Maybe once or twice when we were there, I thought she was sticking her nose in our business, but really not much. How could I say no?"

"Mom had done so much for me," Pam added. "This was something I could do for her."

Ginny's house sold without even going on the market. She gave away a lot of things, stored some more, and the rest she moved into her room at Pam and Ryan's home. Less than a year later, the couple had their first child, a baby girl.

"She still has not left," Ryan stated. "I mean Ginny."

Once Ginny learned of Pam's pregnancy, she made it clear that her travel plans were off. "She told us that she would stay around and help with the housework, the cooking, and of course with the baby after she was born," Pam said.

"Helping is fine, but when it turned into taking over, it became a problem. That is when things started going downhill," Ryan said.

If the baby cried, Ginny would jump up to get her, often moving Ryan out of the way in order to do so.

"She's a slight woman, but seriously, she would literally shove me in the back, then go around me to get to Sara's room," Ryan pointed out.

Ginny told him how to change Sara's diaper, often pushing him aside when she felt Ryan was not doing it correctly.

"It was more than that, and it got worse pretty much every day. She made me feel inept, that whatever I did with Sara was wrong. She moved the dishes around in the kitchen, she went into my stuff and rearranged my underwear and socks," Ryan recounts.

"It did get awkward, I know. Mom found my vibrator once when she was cleaning our room," Pam related.

"And she put it in a different drawer," Ryan imparted. "Yes, you heard that right. She found her daughter's vibrator, picked it up, and moved it to another place."

"I threw it out and got a new one," Pam admitted. "Every time I went to use it, I thought of my mother."

"Not exactly a turn-on," Ryan agreed.

Until the "vibrator incident" as Ryan called it, Pam was not sensing that her mother was interfering or getting into the middle of her marriage:

"I really didn't see it as an issue. But Ryan started snapping at me for what was really no reason," Pam remembers. "I thought she was being helpful really. I didn't care that she did the laundry and tidied up. And helping with the baby was nice—it gave me some time to myself."

"She was really invading our space—not just our physical space, our bedroom, but also our relationship itself. If we had a discussion—almost any discussion— Ginny was around," Ryan noted.

"Once she started coming into our bedroom, going through our things, and making our bed, I certainly understood where Ryan was coming from—that we had some boundary issues that needed fixing," Pam acknowledged.

By that time, though, the couple's relationship was fraying. A new infant brings less sleep, more stress, and less time together even in the best of circumstances.

"I just did not want to deal with Ginny being around for everything at the house," Ryan reiterated. "So I avoided her as much as I could; I would leave the room so I would not have to have another three-way discussion with my mother-in-law and my wife."

"Many times Ryan would eat dinner at his desk at work or even in the car on the way home," Pam observed.

He got up early in the morning so he could spend some time alone with Sara before leaving for the office.

"We were not talking much, and when we did, the conversations were short, there was no real connecting and no intimacy," Pam revealed. "And when he did talk, he was always mad. That of course made me mad and made me not want to initiate any sort of communication or contact."

"I woke up one morning, and Ryan had already left for work," Pam continued. "I decided that we needed to move this thing one way or the other. We were going to make things better or we were going to separate, but I was not going to keep living this way."

That morning, Pam left Sara with Ginny and drove to Ryan's office.

"He was definitely surprised to see me. I walked right in and did not give him a chance to say anything. I gestured for him to get up out from behind his desk, I hugged him, told him I loved him," Pam recounted. "I told him that I knew my mom was getting to be a problem for us and that I was willing to try to fix things if he was."

"Of course I was," Ryan affirmed. "It would have been easy for me to go home that night and tell Ginny that she was wrecking our marriage and she needed to pack her bags."

"The fact was, though, that my mom was not our only problem. We both knew that," Pam pointed out.

The couple decided to go to marriage counseling first and talk to Ginny later after they sorted things out.

"We spent a few months going twice a week. We went once together and also had individual sessions one time each week," Pam described. With some coaching and strategies from the therapist, they confronted Ginny; they told her what was going on and that they thought it best that she move out of the house and find an apartment nearby.

"She cried and said she was sorry. She told us she would do better," Pam disclosed.

"She also told us that she really did not want to move," Ryan added. "And Pam told her it was okay to stay, so she did. She still lives with us. It was not what we had agreed, but knowing Pam's relationship with Ginny, all the time they spent together, I felt like I had to let it go. So I did."

"I could not bring myself to tell her that she had to leave and she would need to live alone," Pam said. "It just was too much for me. Could not do it."

"I understood how difficult it was for Pam," Ryan said. "So I went with it. The two of us sat down with Ginny and tried to talk quietly and unemotionally. We told her that we were willing to try to make it work with her on the housework but there needed to be some general guidelines for us to work with."

"She did not need to do our laundry. And we set Monday and Friday nights as family alone time.

Mom would go out or to her room and watch TV or read a book."

The couple continues to wrestle with Ginny remaining a full-time member of the family.

"She tries to stay out of our way and has not been in our bedroom since then—at least not as far as I know, anyway," Ryan told us. "The stress is there—it's always there, even if a little below the surface. I was not happy that Pam did not do what we had agreed. I do sometimes resent her for that. It still feels as if she put her mother before me and our marriage. But like I said, it was a compromise that I felt I had to make."

Pam and Ryan have continued in counseling, and now rather than getting mad at each other or avoiding each other, they talk through issues when they arise with Ginny.

"And we make our own bed," Pam said.

OUR TAKE

Boundaries, boundaries, boundaries: Everywhere you look, people struggle with boundary issues. For Pam, this started with her mom long before Ryan showed up. "When Pam's father died, Pam became her mom's entire world, her total focus," Julie noted. "She needed that closeness with her mom. And so did Ginny. It worked for both of them in order to get through the loss."

"I am sure there are some people out there who would have killed to have a mother like Ginny, a mom who put her kid first all the time, who wanted to be there with her every step of the way," David interjected.

"I am not trying to minimize Ginny's love for her daughter. Of course she loved her. But the result, at least in part, was that Pam was prevented from individuating, from becoming her own person, in a lot of ways," Julie asserted.

Certainly there may have been attachment issues for Ginny and Pam, but Pam certainly looks like she followed a path and found success. She went to college, got a job, met Ryan, and built a life.

"You've heard me use the term 'enmeshed.' That's what was going on," Julie articulated. "Sure, she went to school, but mom was right there with her. Yes, she met Ryan, but Mom was still there. Even after they had a baby, there is Mom again—making their bed and folding Ryan's underwear. It's not a healthy way to live your life, and while Pam certainly is a successful individual who has a lot to be proud of, she is the first one to point out what she missed out on when she was younger. And why did she miss out on it? Because she felt guilty leaving her mother."

"So it's almost as if Pam and Ginny's lives sort of fused together when Pam's dad died," David mused. "Yes," Julie concurred, "you see this a lot in families where there is some sort of a trauma in the family—which can be an illness, or like here, a death."

For Ginny, there was an enormous gap to fill after her husband died. Pam filled that gap. "And it's not as if Ginny did it purposely or in a mean way. All she did for Pam came from her heart, from a good place," Julie explained. "But unlike some other kids, Pam did not rebel, she did not get into a conflict with her mom or try to push her away."

David calls this an example of the "law of unintended consequences."

"I learned this a long time ago working with people going through a divorce. Many times, the strategies that I discuss with a client—what we are trying to do to reach a particular goal in their case—they can have unintended consequences," David recalled. "Say my client, a mother of a healthy second grader, is ready to move out of the house. She rents a new place, packs her and her son's things, and makes the move. Soon after his parents separate, the boy begins acting out in school and fighting with other kids, not listening, whatever. His behavior after moving with his mother was most certainly nothing she intended or even anticipated. She needed to separate from her husband and get her son in a home without the stress and animosity that was there when everyone was under the same roof. But then the boy acts out and starts causing trouble in school. It was an unintended consequence of the move."

Another unintended consequence was what Julie refers to as "omnipresence." Ginny was what Julie calls "omnipresent" in Pam's life. Pam really preferred that her mother step back, but she did not have the heart to confront her.

"People think of 'omnipresence' as a religious reference—that God is always present, everywhere all the time," Julie clarified. "It's the same idea, just being used differently. Before they got married, Ginny was always around: at the house, in Pam's room, at Pam's games. And when Pam and Ryan married and Ginny moved in, it was the same thing. Those two could not go anywhere without Ginny somehow being present. In some cases it was her physical presence, at every meal, in every room in the house, taking over parenting responsibilities with their daughter. At other times it was just knowing that she had been there, in their room, folding their laundry, that sort of thing. Ginny was always present."

"It had to be so hard for Pam, with her mother having been such a huge part of her life," David reflected, "to find a way to carve out space that did not include Ginny." There were two events that got Pam to make a move. One was when she realized that Ginny was causing trouble in her marriage. The second was when Pam saw that Ginny was taking over the role of mother to Sara. "I have to say, I think it was worse than just taking over, wasn't it? She made Pam feel badly, that she was not a good mom to Sara. And don't forget the whole 'finding her daughter's vibrator' thing. I wouldn't be surprised if Ginny made sure the batteries were fresh for the next time Pam used it."

Julie ignored the last comment. "What really impressed me was that Pam knew she had to act, that she had to do something," Julie emphasized. "She did not talk to Ryan at home with Ginny and other distractions around. She went to his office, and they had a heart to heart right there, just the two of them."

The fact that Pam took the first step really resonated with Ryan. He understood the relationship between Pam and her mom and how tough it was going to be to have the discussion that they both knew they needed to have. That they took a united front and had the conversation with Ginny together was particularly impressive. "Pam probably needed the support, and Ginny certainly had to see clearly that they were on the same page and something needed to change," Julie observed. "It's the same as it is with a child. Parents want to show a united front. In order to make progress, improve the situation, and move forward, Ryan and Pam needed to be on the same page when they talked to Ginny."

Issues surrounding boundaries exist in every relationship: boundaries with children, boundaries with each other and, like Ryan and Pam, boundaries with parents. In all of these relationships, it is important not only to set them, but to check in with some regularity and make sure that they are being adhered to. If not, don't get angry—take a moment, step back and have the discussion in an impassive, more matter-of-fact fashion. Remember, like any important discussion, tone and timing are important. Be respectful, don't yell or raise your voice. Have the conversation at an appropriate time, when there are no distractions or others around.

The couple most definitely took the first step in setting forth and establishing boundaries, with Ginny. Is it smooth sailing from here on out?

"I don't think so," Julie said. "Maintaining those boundaries is going to be another challenge entirely."

Bulitt Point Takeaways

- Communicate regarding family boundaries
- The behavior of others can affect your relationship
- Be mindful of unintended consequences

CHAPTER 10

Pivoting Around Sexual Dysfunction

"I was a little drunk and a lot lonely," Molly revealed right away. "Many of my girlfriends were already married, and a few had babies. Work was great, I had my own place, but I still felt like life was passing me by. I took an Uber to this bar downtown to meet up with my friend and her husband, but they canceled out at the last minute. Since I'd already ordered a glass of wine, I decided to stay for a few minutes, listen to the guy on the piano, and head home for my standard nightcap—Tylenol PM, a book, and bed."

"I was not drunk and certainly not lonely," Ian recounts of the night he and Molly met. "Me and a couple of buddies were roaming from one local spot to another. The boys were drinking, but I drew the short straw and got stuck being designated driver, so it was club soda and a lime for me. We were doing what we liked to do—look for women, see if we could land some action," he said.

"I saw him with some guys at the end of the bar. He had dark hair and a five o'clock shadow and was wearing a beat-up old jean jacket, kind of like one my dad had when I was a kid," Molly continued. "I tried not to stare too much, but I think he caught me at one point; then he came down and squeezed between me and a girl on the barstool to my right, and we just started talking."

Ian starts laughing. "I can't remember the conversation at all—not a word. What I do remember is those legs, the heels; a little gold necklace that dropped down her neck to the center of her chest. All that is clear as day," he declared.

The two left and spent the night together.

"Sex was undoubtedly our initial connection," Molly said. "He made it clear early on that he did not want a monogamous relationship, but I really enjoyed being with him, so I was fine with it. It was your basic 'friends with benefits' relationship."

"I had no intention of getting serious. I liked running around and playing the field. I enjoyed the whole scene—the flirting, the chase, so to speak. And of course the sex. Getting serious with someone was not in my plans at all," Ian discloses. "With Molly, it first started as an hour or two popping in for a drink and sex. Then I started showing up earlier, bringing takeout, and spending the night. A night turned into three nights a week, then long weekends together When I realized that I was in love with Molly, I did not hesitate. I just came out and told her."

Intimacy stayed at the center of their relationship, after they got married and even during Molly's pregnancy.

"Once Molly healed after Jack's birth, we got right back into the swing," Ian smiled.

"I had a high sex drive, and so did Ian. It just was who we were; not one of those couples who had to schedule it once a week or something like that. Having the baby maybe changed when we could do it, but we still did it. We still wanted each other in that way," Molly agreed.

Ten years into the marriage, Ian had a bike accident.

"I was riding early on a Sunday morning, like I always did. It was gorgeous out, sunny with blue skies, and I was just flying along in my own world. I didn't see the pothole on the path before my front tire plowed right in and I went flying over the handlebars. I don't remember much else," Ian related.

Ian broke two ribs and suffered a compound fracture to his leg as well as a concussion.

"What a baby could not do to our sex life, that bike accident took care of," Ian admitted.

"Between the pain medications and the pain," Ian said, "I had no real sense of anything down there. No feeling, no urge. Nothing. I was worried but figured it would go away and I would get back to normal."

"When Ian seemed healthy enough, I sent Jack to my sister's for the night and made us some dinner. While Ian was cleaning up, I went upstairs, took all my clothes off except a pair of heels, and came back to the kitchen," Molly recalls.

"And if I wasn't going to get hard then, it just was not going to happen. She looked amazing. Her body was back like it was before the baby. And those legs— there they were again," Ian emphasized. "We went upstairs, she could not have been sexier or more desirable. She climbed on top of me. Nothing. I had no real sensation at all and nothing close to an erection. After a while, I told her I was sorry and just gave up. Molly traded the heels for slippers and PJ's. We went downstairs and watched some TV."

Ian went to his doctor, who prescribed one medicine after another.

"I went through the whole ED lineup—Viagra, Cialis—most everything that had been approved and even a few that I picked up from internet ads," Ian shared. "Nothing worked."

Ian's inability to have sex did not diminish his desire for intimacy.

"I wanted it but did not know what else I could do that would help. At one point, I half joked to my buddy that if things did not improve, he might have to take care of Molly for me. He made a crack along the lines of 'that's what friends are for' or something like that," Ian remembers.

Despite Ian's concern for Molly and his ability to joke about it with his friends, Ian's mood began to darken.

"He was angry a lot, short with me and not all that interested in spending time with Jack," Molly acknowledged. "I tried to be sympathetic, but it got to the point where his attitude really pissed me off. I mean, I understood the sex issue and how he felt guilty or maybe somehow less of a man. But our relationship was more than that. We were best friends and parents to this wonderful boy. I felt that if Ian would just forget about it for a while, he could enjoy the other parts of his life and eventually the sex piece would get better."

"I did not think that marriage counseling was the answer. The issue was me and how it was all affecting me. I knew it and so did Molly. I just could not figure out how to get out of where I was. I did not mean for my penis to run my life, but it sort of was doing just that," Ian concedes.

Molly suggested to Ian that he should talk it through with someone who was not directly involved. She convinced him to find his own therapist.

"I really did not want to go, but I did not know what else to try at that point. So I went—on my own, not with Molly," Ian clarified. "I was surprised but I liked it. I liked talking to Stephanie and felt like she was listening, not judging or criticizing me. Not that Molly had been critical, but she definitely was fed up with how the entire situation was affecting our relationship."

"I heard a lot about Stephanie," Molly commented. "He talked a lot about what went on in their sessions. I was hopeful."

"Stephanie talked to me a lot about mindfulness; how I should experience sex in the moment, let it happen without judging or being critical of myself," Ian went on. "She convinced me that my inability to have an erection did not mean that Molly and I could not have sexual encounters."

Ian bought some toys for the couple to try in the bedroom. He and Molly used them together.

"I liked it, I felt it was nice that he thought of me. He liked to watch. For me, that was very sexy. It gave me what I needed physically. It was fun and enjoyable for me," Molly affirms.

"Me too," Ian agreed.

With some more input from the therapist, Molly and Ian also started doing new activities together. They went camping with Jack on weekends and learned how to play pickleball. Molly took up golf.

"That is when something happened," Ian elucidated. "I was having a beer while Molly was taking a lesson from the pro up at the public course near us. He was putting his arms on Molly's hips, helping her learn to turn during the golf swing. Nothing sexual about it, but I started to feel it again. Desire."

"Horny is what you mean," Molly interjects.

"That's it, yes. It was a good feeling," Ian concurred.

A few years have passed, and the couple has settled into a consistent and comfortable sex life. "It's not like when we could not keep our hands of each other, but it's still good," Molly offers.

"I'm the Toby Keith lyric. I'm not as good as I once was," Ian said. Molly smiles and finishes for him.

"But you're as good once as you ever were."

OUR TAKE

"This was a hard one," David observed.

"Very funny. I knew that was coming," Julie admitted. "We joke, but this is not something that couples find easy to talk about—with each other or anyone else."

For many people, sex is a vital and necessary part of a relationship. It can either help to drive a couple to be happier or cause them to drift apart. For Ian and Molly, sex had been a major connector in their relationship from the outset. It is equally important to both of them.

"I talk a lot about how libido is like thirst. People have different thirst levels," Julie explained. "I need to drink more during the day than you do, for example. The same is true with sex drives. With Ian and Molly, their sex drives match up."

"Simpatico in bed, so to speak," David added. "And let's be honest. Doesn't that make a relationship easier? Seriously, if you are in a room with a hundred couples and all of them have fulfilling sex lives, I don't think too many are going to say they are unhappy in their relationship."

There are certainly other areas of importance in a relationship. But if a couple has a healthy sexual relationship, that eliminates one significant area of frequent conflict and struggle. "That's not to say that Ian and Molly did not have other relationship complications, but other than Ian's accident, we sure did not hear much about those," Julie pointed out. "There was some talk about her disappointment in Ian in terms of his withdrawing both from Molly and their son Jack. Also they both seemed to agree that Ian became short-tempered and uncommunicative. But their focus most definitely was on the sex."

This is just another example of what we talk about all the time. Everyone is different; every relationship is different. What is a primary focus for one couple may not even be on the radar for another. Some couples don't have sex at all, for example, for whatever reason—health, lack of drive or interest, there can be many reasons. But those couples can have successful and long-lasting relationships.

"Ian's therapist did some really good work," Julie notes. "She was able to get Ian to move past all the negative feelings he was having about not being able to perform—the embarrassment, the guilt. She also got him to take his foot off the pedal when it came to putting pressure on himself."

Arriving at an understanding of how mindfulness could help him sexually was a real success for Ian. Ian needed to be fully present and aware of what was bringing on his insecurity and not be reactive regarding what he was unable to do physically in the moment. "There are techniques and strategies—even apps—that therapists recommend to clients in order for someone to push more focus into the present, attending to what is there at that time and not what is not," Julie elucidated.

Both couples had to put in the work to move forward. For Molly, it was patience and understanding. Her desire for sex had not waned, but she was able to be kind and express empathy for Ian in a way that lessened his feelings of inadequacy. It is one thing for a therapist to give advice and provide a patient with techniques and tools. For all of that to work, the client has to follow that advice and implement those strategies. Ian did that.

Bulitt Point Takeaways

- Sex drives can be like thist; individuals' needs vary as to both
- Be present in the moment with your partner
- A therapist can provide useful tools to a couple experiencing intimacy issues

CHAPTER 11

Living with Bipolar Disorder

Bipolar disorder is a mental health condition that causes extreme mood swings. Genetics, an altered brain structure, and even environmental circumstances all may contribute to causing the disorder.

"Yes, I have done a lot of reading on the subject," said Jim, who is an IT director for a midsized company. "It's also known as manic depression."

He and Laura first met at a wedding when they were in their mid-thirties. Jim was friends with the groom; Laura was the bride's coworker. Up to that point, neither of them had been in a serious relationship.

"We were introduced during the reception, and Laura started talking right away. She was outgoing and really friendly. She laughed a lot," Jim recalled.

They went on a few dates over the next couple of months. "We went to movies and dinner, the basic stuff," Jim went on. "She was just great to be around."

"We were hitting it off, and I did not want it to go further without Jim knowing about my disease," Laura explains. "I did not want to waste his time or mine if it was going to be a problem. It was not the first time that I had liked someone and decided to tell them that I was bipolar, just so they knew what they were getting into. Up until Jim came along, that was the end of any possible relationships. As soon as I told the guy I was bipolar, a date got postponed but never rescheduled or was canceled altogether. A couple of times, I just got stood up and never heard from the guy again."

"I was fine with it. She said that she had bad days now and again, but with the medicine she was on, her symptoms were usually no big deal. After we got serious and I decided that I was going to ask her to marry me, I called my family and let them know. I told them about Laura being bipolar," Jim revealed. "I grew up in Nebraska. I know it must have sounded scary to both my parents. They told me that I was making a big mistake, that I should break up with her and run."

"We have been married almost fifteen years now and he is still here," Laura voiced softly.

Jim and Laura talked through Laura's illness at length before they got married.

"I was very open about it," Laura remembered. "Even though he knew about it, he needed to know what it might mean for him as a husband and maybe a father."

"She made sure I went along to talk to her psychiatrist. The doctor explained Laura's medications, what could happen if she went off them, symptoms to look for," Jim noted. "I knew what was getting into."

After a couple of years, the couple decided that they wanted to have children.

"Things between us were great," Laura recounted. "We didn't fight much; our lives were calm and quiet. I was happy and not having any real issues with my health. It just felt like it was the time to add to our family."

It took a while for Laura to get pregnant. "We tried every month, but nothing for a year at least. Then, boom, we have twins coming," Jim emphasized.

What Jim did not know was that early in her pregnancy, Laura had stopped taking her medications. At first, Jim did not notice any change in her behavior.

"Honestly, I did not think about it anymore. She was not having any of the episodes or symptoms that I'd been warned about, so I guess I just thought she was better."

"I was worried about the effects of the medications on the babies, so I decided to stop taking them," Laura articulated.

She did not discuss it with her psychiatrist.

"And I did not tell Jim because I knew he would want me back on the medications. I was not going to take those pills and jeopardize the health of my babies. It was one of those 'ends justifies the means' kind of things."

It was not long after the twins were born that Laura began experiencing postpartum depression.

"I wanted to nurse, but it did not work with either of the girls. They both screamed and seemed to push my breast away," Laura recalls. "Jim had to bottle-feed them, and I just went back to bed."

"Laura—she cried a lot. When she was not crying or sleeping, she yelled at me and the twins too," Jim observed. "Her diet was basically Gatorade, Diet Coke, a yogurt here or there, and some coffee."

Jim found out on his own that Laura was off her medications.

"I was going through the medicine cabinet and noticed that each of the bottles was dated from several months earlier," he related. "I asked her about it, and she told me that she had to go off to protect the babies. I learned that Laura had not seen or even spoken with her psychiatrist in over six months. I was pissed that she'd lied to me, but by then that was not the point. Since she was not nursing, any risk to the babies from the medications was gone. She needed to get back on her medications, and I told her so."

Laura refused.

The manic phase of her disorder kicked in. "She stopped sleeping. One night she would be vacuuming the house at two in the morning. The next night she might be painting the front door," Jim continued. "She would be blasting music downstairs, singing in the middle of the night with the kids asleep and me trying to get some sleep. It would go on for several days, maybe a week. Then all of a sudden she would be back to sleeping and crying. She told me many times that the girls did not love her."

With Laura toggling between mania and depression while refusing to get back on her medications, and with two infants in the home and Jim needing to be able to function at work, he made two decisions. The first was to call his mother, who flew in from Nebraska to help with the babies. The second was to present Laura with an ultimatum.

"The girls were close to their first birthday, and we had been living with this for too long. They did not know their mother very well, and what they did know frightened them. Every day was potluck. I never knew what to expect. Was Laura going to be depressed and sleep the day away in the dark? Or was some mania going to keep her up all night compulsively doing something around the house that did not need to be done? I told her that she needed to get help, or I was leaving with the girls and moving to Nebraska. There was no other choice."

"At first I told him to go ahead and get the hell out," Laura interjects. "I thought he would be better off without me—the girls too."

"After that first conversation, I almost did leave," Jim acknowledged. "My mom was there. She heard the entire conversation. I went upstairs and pulled the suitcases out of the attic. I was ready to go right then, I really was. My mom convinced me to wait, let a couple of days pass, and try talking to her again. The same woman who told me to run before we got married was now telling me to stay put."

Jim did stay, and a week later he and Laura talked again, this time without emotion and threats. "He told me that the girls loved me and that I could be a good mom to them," Laura imparted. "I did not want them to go."

The two went together to Laura's psychiatrist and filled her in on what had been happening at home. The psychiatrist prescribed Laura medications to treat the bipolar disease. Laura also agreed that it would be best for the family to move to Nebraska, where they would have more family support.

"I did not want Jim and the girls to have to go it alone if I had another episode," Laura expressed. Jim could keep his job and work remotely from Nebraska. "We got a referral to a new doctor in Omaha who we met with on Zoom before the move." The new psychiatrist told Laura that she wanted her in therapy regularly and asked Laura to sign a consent form that would authorize her to speak directly with Jim.

"I wanted my family to stay a family. If it meant more therapy and that the doctor or therapist was permitted to talk to Jim, that was okay with me," Laura affirmed.

Since the move to Omaha, Laura has been able to stay active in the girls' lives. She was a room mom at the elementary school and helped coach soccer. Even though she has stayed on her medications, Laura still struggles with depression.

"The therapy has helped with the mood swings, and the drugs have kept the manic episodes to a minimum," Laura stated. "But the depression piece, that is tough. I deal with it a lot."

Despite the move to Nebraska and Laura being fully compliant with her medications and doctor's recommendations, her relationship with Jim changed permanently after the children were born.

"We have never been able to go back to those early days of being freer and easier with each other," Laura reflected. "I think he lost some trust, and although I am working on it—and it is work, every single day—I still feel as if that trust has not come back and never will."

"We don't live in fear, I would not say that," Jim clarified, "but it is always there, and that has made for some difficult times in our marriage. I suppose that it is like living with an alcoholic. You just don't know when she might fall off the wagon. But we are bonded together with our history and our children. Neither of us wants to leave."

"Staying married to Jim, no matter how hard it can be at times, is still better than not being married to Jim," Laura agreed.

OUR TAKE

A person who is bipolar can be extremely difficult to connect with, much less be married to. "I kept wondering how Jim was able to hang in and stick with her," David commented.

Genetics can be a cause of bipolar disease. "There is some research out there that suggests that when some people are born, they are more prone to developing bipolar disorder," Julie pointed out. "It's basically caused by chemical imbalances in the brain—the chemicals themselves are called neurotransmitters. Neurotransmitters control the brain's functions."

Roughly 40 percent of the adults in the US report that they struggle with substance abuse or mental health issues. And if you apply that number to couples, there is a pretty good chance that at least one of the two people in the relationship will experience one or both.

"It's the mood swings with Laura that I just don't know if I could handle. One day she's up and doing, the next the shades are pulled and she is buried under the blankets," David articulated. "How do you find a way to get along, much less be a team and raise a family with all that going on?"

"Bipolar disease is complicated and difficult both for the sufferer and their friends or family," Julie added. "The mood swings, the pendulum of ups and downs—it is all very tough to manage. Bipolar is more common than you might think. But as you heard from Laura and Jim, there are medications that can be very effective."

Keeping someone with bipolar disease on their medications can also prove to be difficult. Often what happens is that when someone has been feeling well, then they think they don't need the medicine anymore and just stop cold turkey.

"This can bring on a manic or a depressive phase, and then it is more difficult to reach the person—to get them to see what is going on and go back on the medications," Julie explained.

Laura seemingly had a good reason to go off the medication. Many medications can be harmful to a pregnant mother and her child.

"But Laura should have told Jim that she was going off the medications. They should have had a discussion about it," Julie stressed. "At the very least— even if he disagreed—he would have been more prepared emotionally for the consequences. And there are some doctors who would have advised her to stay on the medication during the pregnancy, that the mother's health should be the primary concern."

"It was quite a difference from when they first met," David noted. "Remember? Laura told Jim about her being bipolar right at the beginning of their relationship. She was up-front—maybe too much so if you ask me. But later, she goes off the medications and keeps it all a secret."

Julie thinks that came down to familiarity from their time spent together. "At the beginning, Laura liked Jim. She wanted to see if they could have a future. Intellectually, she thought it made sense to be totally transparent and up-front. They had been married and together a good while by the time Laura got pregnant. She thought she could keep going off her medication a secret and at that point was not worried about the consequences."

"Laura had a lot more at risk then than when they first started dating, although I guess she did not see it that way," David reasoned. "You have got to admire Jim for how he took over the situation after the twins were born."

Jim was working in uncharted territory for sure. He could not have known what Laura's response would be to him bringing his mother into their house to basically take over a lot of her responsibilities, as well as his telling her he was moving to Nebraska and taking the kids. He forced her into a decision without having any sense of her response.

"He listened to Mr. Spock," David elucidated. "It's a great line from that Star Trek movie, *The Wrath of*

Khan. 'The needs of the many outweigh the needs of the few, or the one.' Jim was forced to make a really difficult decision, but he stepped up and he made it. His children's needs outweighed Laura's needs."

"So true," Julie agreed. "I love that. Laura ultimately understood that Jim was serious and that she too had to make a decision. It was a brave one—moving across the country. But she did it."

"There are a couple of things I want to mention here. First, the lawyer in me says that Jim should have thought long and hard about getting a Prenuptial Agreement done before they got married," David said. "Discussing what happens if we divorce is not particularly romantic and rarely an easy discussion to have when people are planning a wedding, but for Jim, much of what he was worried about—finances, potentially issues surrounding the children—could have been managed a long time before Laura's mental health struggles resurfaced. At this point though, Jim decides he has to give Laura an ultimatum—you do this or I will do that—a strategy that generally is not useful. It does not work with kids, and it is rarely effective when it comes to my work in divorce settlement negotiations."

And ultimatums rarely work in relationships either. When they do work, it's usually because a person is afraid of being abandoned in some way. "That is exactly what played out here," Julie concluded. "Laura was scared of being alone, without Jim and the children. Maybe also scared of being left alone with her disease."

Is it possible that Laura will eventually grow to resent Jim for trying to control her by presenting her with that ultimatum?

"I don't see Jim's having forced Laura to make a choice here as being a power move or an attempt to control her," David stated. "His intent was to save his family, to keep his marriage together and his kids safe and healthy. To me what he did was an act of courage, not an attempt to control his wife."

"The real question, though," Julie wondered, "is not what Jim's intent was, but how did Laura interpret the choice that Jim forced her to make?"

Bulitt Point Takeaways

- Be open with your partner from the outset of the relationship
- Bipolar disease is treatable
- Giving an ultimatum to your partner is likely to be harmful to a relationship

CHAPTER 12

Bending to Gender Fluidity

Megan was twenty-seven when friends introduced her to Lynn—then Lukas—at a birthday party for a mutual friend.

"It sounds so clichéd, I know, but we had an instant connection," Lynn reminisced. "She was certainly pretty, but when we started talking, it was as if we'd known each other forever—love at first sight for sure."

"He was beautiful. Really. And I say 'he' because that is what I saw when we met," Megan recalled; "this tall, beautiful man."

"I was a few years older when we met, and I had been in the singles scene for a while," Lynn recounts. "I realized back when I was in Oklahoma that I was bisexual, and when I got to Philadelphia, it was more comfortable. I was active sexually with both men and women."

Lynn's life growing up could not be more different than the life she leads now.

"Like I said, I was raised in Oklahoma, in a small town outside of Tulsa. I don't think I even saw a Jewish person until I came east," Lynn pointed out. "Tulsa is a pretty conservative place, and I really never fit in. I had some friends growing up, but not too many. High school was tough for me particularly as I had a lot of contradictory feelings in terms of who I was, my attraction to both men and women, and why I was not like my siblings."

Lynn's family was not upset when she left and moved to Philadelphia.

"I was the youngest of three, and both my brother and sister were really popular all through school," Lynn explained. "My brother went on to get his degree in engineering from OU. He is still single and has a great job now. My sister got married and is raising her kids about a mile from where we grew up. All very neat and perfect, right?"

"Things were so different with me," Lynn continued. "They knew I was different; I did not talk much about school, I was not an athlete or anything else really. I stayed to myself, and I don't think I ever brought a friend home. I liked my mom's magazines—*Home and Garden*, *Southern Living*. Saturdays in the fall were really the worst for me. Early in the morning, we would meet up with the neighbors at someone's house, eat, and get ready for the OU football game," she said. "We would spend the whole day sitting, throwing a ball around, and watching the game, then more food and drinking after the game. Most times we did not get home until really late. I tried to find a quiet place to sit—out of the way so no one would notice. I hated everything about those Saturdays— the crowd of people, the food, the screaming, the yelling—all of it. After high school, I started painting my nails, coloring my hair, and dressing differently. They were relieved when I told them I was leaving. I have not been back since."

"My story is not nearly as exciting," Megan stressed. "I'm a Jewish girl from Philly. I grew up in Lower Merion with mostly Jewish families, went to Hebrew School, had my Bat Mitzvah, and got confirmed at Adath Israel. I was twenty-seven when we met, and my sex life was fairly nonexistent. Sure, I had slept with a few guys, but nothing particularly memorable. I wanted to experience more but did not know how to put myself out there without it being weird or feeling like I was loose."

The pair dated for over a year before deciding to get married.

"When we first had sex, I thought, 'Oh my God, so this is what I had been missing'," Megan revealed. "We did a lot of different things sexually, and we also brought others into our bed with us. For me it was all new. I knew Lynn—then Lukas—had done a lot that I had not, and I enjoyed having him show me."

"We continued having sex with others for a good while; sometimes couples, sometimes just one person—gay and straight, men and women," Lynn went on. "Our life together was great, but I was starting to feel like I did when I was in Oklahoma, like there was something I was missing. I woke up one morning and looked at myself in the mirror. Something did not feel right to me. I did not feel right. I was not who I should be."

"I came home from work one night. We had been married about eight years. Lukas—still Lukas to me at that point—he was in our bedroom with a dress on," Megan remembered. "It was one of my work dresses from Saks that was way too short for him. No shoes, but makeup and hair all slicked back like one of those '60s models. Very pretty."

"I sat on the bed and told her that I was trans, that I was supposed to be a woman," Lynn added; "that I needed to change but I did not want our relationship to change."

"We were happy, and I did not see why that should change because Lukas was going to be Lynn. She was the same person to me. I was fine with the whole gender-fluid thing and perfectly comfortable if this was what Lynn felt she needed," Megan affirmed. "We stayed in the lifestyle and continued to go to the couples parties like before. It was no different except now I was going with Lynn instead of Lukas. What I didn't expect, though, was Lynn getting into a relationship with one of the women we met soon after she transitioned."

"Our relationship was open from Day One," Lynn emphasized. "We each were free to have sex with other people so long as we told the other and were honest about our feelings. I told Megan about Jill the night we met. There was no secret that I felt something more for Jill than others I had been with. It was not an option to keep that to myself."

"Sometimes it's better not to know, maybe," Megan reflected. "I mean, I understand it is important to be honest in a relationship, and with ours being how it was—honesty and trust were necessary. If they had just had sex, then we went home like usual, it would have been no big deal. But she was so matter-of-fact about it, you know? Lynn was like, 'Listen, I met this woman Jill. I really have feelings for her.' No emotion. 'This is how it is, and that's that' kind of thing."

"I was following our rules," Lynn reiterated.

"I understand. But it was hard for me. Not the sex obviously. The feelings. That hurt," Megan expressed.

"I love Megan. I have feelings for Jill also. Maybe it's love, maybe it isn't. We are figuring that out," Lynn imparted. "None of it should affect how Megan and I are together though. We are married. We have a life together. This is just a part of it—a part we both agreed to from the beginning."

"See, this is what she says all the time. 'This is what we agreed to' and 'Nothing has changed.' It has changed," Megan asserted. "Sex is an instant kind of gratification—you lust, you want it, you get it, and then you're done. But she is never done with Jill, and it does get in the way of our time together, our life together."

"That is only because you let it get in the way," Lynn maintained.

"I have a lot of trouble with Lynn's attitude. Really, I do. Where was Jill when she transitioned? Where was Jill when she lost her job and spent three days in bed? The answer is easy—not around. That was all me. I stood by her through everything. I dealt with the trauma her transitioning caused to my relationship with my family. I could have walked away and left her and gone on with my life. It would have been a hell of a lot easier, I can tell you," Megan shared.

It has been three years since Lynn transitioned and began her relationship with Jill.

"It is hard for me every day. But I love her and am trying to keep this jealousy thing at bay. I want Lynn to be happy, and if having Jill in her life is part of that, then I need to figure it out if I want us to stay together," Megan concluded.

"She does," Lynn said. "She will."

OUR TAKE

The two of us see this relationship and its future differently. For David, it looks like too many couples he has seen in his office, while Julie sees the different roles couples take and can successfully navigate.

Lynn spoke for quite a while before allowing Megan to get a word in edgewise.

"Keep in mind that a high percentage of trans people are on the autism spectrum," Julie noted. "That could explain her going on and on."

This relationship, superficially at least, comes across as very one-sided. "Lynn does not take responsibility for anything. It's Megan who has to adjust, make changes, understand things. Lynn does not accept any responsibility," David articulated.

Although Lynn does strike us as selfish, it is not at all unusual for someone on the spectrum to have an inability to understand or perceive what someone else is feeling. "Sorry. She is selfish. It's all about her, what she wants, what she needs," David averred. "There was a complete refusal to grasp that what she does can affect Megan and their relationship. Being on the spectrum might be a reason, but it should not be an excuse."

"Their relationship has a lot of layers to it," Julie commented. "The trans piece that came after they were married and Lynn's autism spectrum disorder both have continuing impacts on their relationship."

A lot of layers? For sure. Transgender and autism. "Add on the open marriage agreement, and now a girlfriend for Lynn. It's a lot for them to handle," David said.

There is evidence that the divorce rate for people in open marriages is higher than for other marriages. There is a reason for that. "Of course there is," Julie voiced. "We are human beings. We have emotions and feelings. One of those emotions is jealousy. For people in open relationships, things are usually fun, exciting, and interesting. Bringing in new partners or multiple partners can be very enticing sexually to some people. But over time, it can get complicated, like it did here with Megan and Lynn. What we see with them paints it clear as day—sharing your partner sexually and emotionally has its disadvantages."

Megan is particularly easygoing, as she tells it. She professes just to want Lynn to be happy. If Lynn is happy, then Megan is happy. "Sorry, but I am not buying it," David declared. "First, this small-town Jewish girl meets a man that she is immediately attracted to. She likes the whole open relationship thing. That part I can understand. But the rest of it? No way. There is an explosion on the horizon."

We both frequently see this dynamic in our practices: One spouse says the same thing Megan said—"whatever she wants is fine with me"—no opinion, just going with the flow. The other spouse runs the show—whatever they say goes. At some point, there is bound to be an "I have had enough" moment, and then, as David put it, is when that explosion is going to happen. "And I will bet you a week's pay it is going to happen with Megan," David went on.

And what about the impact of the loss Megan must have felt when Lynn told her about needing to live as a female? Megan most certainly had to feel something, but she did not express it to Lynn. She held her feelings in, stayed quiet, and avoided any potential conflict.

"And after all of that, now we have Lynn basically forcing Megan into a polyamorous relationship," David observed. "It's part of the same pattern. Lynn unilaterally controls the very nature of the relationship. She directs every aspect of their lives. Think about it—Lynn says let's have sex with other people, Megan says yes. Lynn says I need to be a female. Megan says sure. Now, Lynn says for all intents and purposes, 'I want to have a relationship with another person too—not just a quickie, and you need to accept it.' This time, though, Megan has reservations. She expresses a desire to figure it out and come to grips with it, but she is not fully accepting of the situation."

"Megan and Lynn have been together for a long time. While you want to focus on all that Megan has sacrificed to make the relationship work, I think you are missing something very basic between these two," Julie responded. "It is working—for them. They have been together—and I say 'they' because it is both of them. We both know that every relationship is different. What works for one couple does not work for another. And while Lynn is demanding—no doubt about it—Megan seems not just accepting of that trait but comfortable with it. We talk about looking into what makes relationships work, right? This relationship works because both are comfortable in their respective roles—with Lynn the more dominant of the two and Megan more passive. Both are comfortable and accepting of their roles, and that right there is their glue. That is what keeps them together—for over ten years now and counting."

"I just don't think you are going to have to count much higher," David offered.

Bulitt Point Takeaways

- Jealousy can arise in any relationship
- A person's perspective is often their reality
- Each relationship is unique; what works in one relationship may not work for another

CHAPTER 13

Finding Trust and
Learning to Forgive

Carly walked in with a copy of *The Five Core Conversations* in tow. "He is not much of a reader. I read a chapter or two at a time and highlight the parts I want him to read," she began.

Holden sat down on a rolling chair and grabbed a couple of the fidget toys usually reserved for Julie's younger clients. "I will do better if I can move around," he expressed.

"Maybe we should sit together on the couch?" Carly asked.

Holden stayed in the rolling chair. Carly sat down in the chair next to him. Hers did not roll.

Holden is thirty-five and has been working in landscaping "on and off" for the last ten years.

"There were a lot of times that I was not working," Holden clarified. "My parents got divorced after being married for thirty years. I was twenty-five and had just met Carly. My dad met another woman and ran off with her."

Holden did not handle his parents' divorce well.

"I started drinking and drugging," Holden recalled; "pills during the daytime, alcohol at night."

"I come from a family of long-term relationships," Carly shared. "My parents have been married for more than forty years and my grandparents over sixty."

Raised as a Messianic Jew, Carly was homeschooled by her mother and then went on to be a nurse.

"It's basically Judaism, only that we believe Jesus to be the Messiah," Carly explained. "There is more to it, but that is the biggest difference."

Carly got pregnant while she was in school.

"My parents urged me to get married. They said it was the right thing for the baby," she recounted. "So I went through with it, but from the start—as I was saying the vows—it just did not feel right."

Carly and her first husband separated soon after their daughter, Bianca, had her first birthday.

"He hasn't been in the picture since then," Carly said of her first husband.

While on her way to work one morning, Carly ran into Holden. The two had previously been introduced by Holden's younger brother.

"He was good looking and sweet, so I called his brother and got his number," Carly related. "He asked me if I was sure about wanting to get to know Holden better, that his brother was 'a real a**hole.' I laughed and told him I liked a challenge."

"She was beautiful, and I liked her from the start. I'm glad she called me. We probably would not have gotten together otherwise," Holden mused.

The couple dated for several months before moving in together. Soon after, Carly got pregnant, and the couple had a son.

"Everything seemed to be fine until Holden got his DUI," Carly asserted. "Drug dealers were coming to our place all the time, and that was when I realized Holden had a problem.

It kept getting worse, with him high a lot, sometimes he was home, a lot of times not."

"She moved out while I was asleep," Holden interjects.

"I had two young kids, and I was not going to risk their safety because of him," Carly emphasized. "I packed and hid suitcases the night before. My dad helped me set up an apartment for me and the kids. I thought we were done. I did go back to our place once after the move to take the couches. He called me after, screaming and yelling. He did not understand why I took them."

It was a long time before Holden saw the children again.

"I was an addict, and that was how I was living. When I started with heroin, that is really when I went downhill," Holden acknowledges.

"He came over one night and was clean, or maybe I just wanted it to seem that way," Carly added. "The kids were asleep, and I invited him in. I loved him still and wanted him too."

The two had sex that night.

"Sex has always been amazing," Carly disclosed. "It was something we both wanted and has always kept us connected through both good times and bad ones."

"We went back and forth like that for a long time. I would get clean, Carly and I would spend some time together, and then I would relapse again," Holden said.

"It was a cycle. He would move back in with us for a while, then I would have to throw him out because of the drugs. We fought a lot, but I could not put an end to things. I handled it by drinking and smoking a lot of weed," Carly described.

Although Holden was able to get back to work, his struggles continued.

"I got three more DUIs and then stole money from my boss. I wrote a bunch of checks to myself," Holden said.

"At that point, I made a decision," Carly stated. "I told him straight up, 'If you can't do this, let me know and get out of our way. Allow us to be loved by someone else.'"

After five months in jail, Holden went into a recovery program, got his job back, and began attending church.

"I reached out to Carly and asked if she would come to church with me," Holden noted.

The couple started attending church and AA meetings together.

"I needed some help too. I was still drinking and smoking. It was a good opportunity for me to get some help and get it with Holden. I admit that I was a little gun-shy about starting to see him again after all we had been through. It was not easy, I can tell you. Even though she was little, my daughter still remembers a lot of those bad times—the fighting, Holden coming and going. He was living out back in an old broken down shed because I would not let him come into the house."

"I was thankful that she was willing to give me another chance with her and our family," Holden shared.

"We both got cleaned up. He is an awesome dad to both of the kids. My daughter thinks of Holden as her father," Carly said. "We do laugh a lot now. We also argue and bicker all the time, but we get over it. And the sex is still great."

"It is. It helps us patch over rough spots," Holden concurred.

"Sometimes it seems like the only time we aren't arguing or disagreeing is when we are having sex," Carly laughed. "We communicate very differently, and sometimes that is a problem. He generally does not want to talk about things. I am actually surprised he agreed to come and talk to you."

"She doesn't let me get away with anything," Holden admitted. "If I am out of line, she calls me on it and tells me straight up what I did wrong, and how to make it right."

"I come from a family where we talk about everything. It can be loud and hard, but that is how I was raised," Carly affirmed.

"We got married in 2018," Carly went on. "I felt at that time that Holden was over the addictions, that we could count on him. Once I got to that point, marrying him was absolutely the right thing. When we got married, my dad told me that he always knew there was a good man hiding in Holden, he just did not know if that good man would come out."

"I am in a different place, and it feels really good," Holden expressed.

The couple and their kids are living with Carly's parents to save money for a house.

"That is a little tough, but hopefully it won't last too long," Holden commented. "Living with her mom and dad, that can be tough on everyone—me, Carly, the kids. Her parents also, I am sure."

Not surprisingly, Carly and Holden also parent differently.

"I am clearer cut and get to the point," Holden clarified. "Carly is quieter and much more patient most of the time. When we disagree about something with the kids, I really try to speak in a softer voice. It's not what you say, it's how you say it, right?"

"See, he does read your book," Carly pointed out. "Our life together can be tumultuous, but it is never boring. But now I know that I can count on him. He loves our family, and I know in my heart that with God's help, we will be okay."

"I do believe that God has a plan for us. Carly has helped me to become another, better person," Holden affirmed.

"When I look at our lives together," Carly concluded, "I really see two different canvasses—two different paintings. One is when Holden was on drugs—that one is very dark with black and grays. The other is our life since he has been clean. It's pretty and bright, all vibrant and colorful."

OUR TAKE

Carly described her relationship with Holden as "two canvasses." She has such a clear grasp on her life, where she came from, and where she wants to go.

"Carly was young. She made some bad choices for sure, getting pregnant at such a young age, then marrying someone that she knew was not right for her," Julie observed.

Her relationship with Holden also sprang a bit from impulsivity. They dated, she already had one child, and then they moved in together. "It wasn't overnight, but it was not a real long time either," David notes. "I was thinking that she might have taken her time more and been more protective of her daughter—and herself for that matter. It just does not seem to fit with how she seems in such control now."

"First of all, Carly is a grown-up now. She has had real-life experiences—and not easy ones. She was not fully formed in a lot of ways when she got pregnant and married the first time," Julie stressed. "Today, we see this confident woman who is strong and mature. I am sure that we would have seen a different Carly if we had spoken with her fifteen years ago."

By the time Holden was drowning in drug addiction, Carly had developed a strength that she did not have earlier in her life. She walled him away from her and the children. It could not have been easy, but she did what she had to do; she said to herself, "I am not going to live this way, I am not going to let my kids live this way," packed up, and got out. And for Holden, regaining Carly's trust was a part of his recovery.

"This is a good example of your view about sex in a relationship, of how it can grease the wheels," Julie mused.

"I think their attraction to each other most definitely helped build a bridge for the two of them, a vessel kind of for Carly to feel more comfortable thinking about trusting him again," David reasoned. "I think we can agree that sex may not be the only thing or even necessarily the most important thing between two people. I do think that if a couple is satisfied sexually, then it gives them a better chance of getting through the difficulties that we all face. These two have that chemistry and connection, and I think it helped the process."

"Carly said it herself—the sex is always great, and they both wanted it. So when Holden got out of jail, got clean, and started going to church and maintaining his sobriety, Carly was more open to re-establishing a relationship for sure. Sleeping together brought them closer," Julie elucidated. "There was not the pressure of sexual disharmony that can cause difficulty in relationships—here it was quite the opposite. The sex helped them connect and kept them close physically, and that in turn helped them find their way back together as a couple."

But that was not all that it took to get these two on the right path. Regaining the trust did not happen overnight. "The first thing that both of them had to do was to commit to each other and their relationship," Julie asserted. "They both had to take responsibility for what had caused the break to begin with. And I mean Carly too."

"You mean maybe turning a blind eye at first to the addiction, maybe not trying hard enough to get Holden the help he needed before she made the choice to move out," David interjected.

Carly also made the decision that she was going to try to let go of the difficult times and memories of the past and move forward. Attending support meetings and church together was a way that the two of them started to look forward and in a way began to create new memories—doing that together was a new and different kind of intimacy for them. At that point, they were both committed to repairing their relationship.

"When you have a partner, friend, relative—anyone really—who has an addiction, it has to be difficult not to cross the line between supporting that person and enabling them," David said. "It appears to me that Carly figured that out and did a terrific job of supporting Holden in his recovery without enabling his addiction. They did things together, he was slowly welcomed back into the family. But if there was a relapse, a slip off the rail, he knew he would be was back in the shed."

"Relationships that can endure—the ones where people are able to work through complicated and trying conflict or trauma—those relationships strengthen, and the feelings for each other get more intense," Julie averred.

Are the frequent arguments a symptom of that increased intensity?

"I am not saying that the relationship has gotten more intense," Julie articulated. "You and I love each other—and I would like to think that is a lasting love, but intense? No, I would not describe our relationship in that way. What we see with Carly and Holden— their feelings for each other have this certain intensity about them. It comes out both in their arguing and their sexual relationship."

"I see that," David responded. "Often you talk about people having to be in the right place emotionally to have sex. If someone is not in a good place with their partner—they are not communicating well or there is something else causing conflict with their partner—either the partner doesn't want to have sex or it's not fulfilling. With Carly and Holden, that aspect of intimacy is there regardless of what is happening in the rest of their relationship."

In order for them to stay together and move forward, however, Holden first had to get himself together. Carly was not opening that door unless he did. Holden had to get into recovery and stay there.

"Carly was firm about that for sure," Julie acknowledged. "He may have come into her bed now and again, but he was not getting back into the house and the family without getting clean. He would have stayed in that old shed."

And they would have stayed on the dark side of the canvas.

Bulitt Point Takeaways

- There is power in forgiveness
- Sex is one way to stay connected, but not the only way
- Trust can be regained, but often needs to be earned

CHAPTER 14

Keeping the Faith
Through Infertility

Beth does not really like talking about the four plus years of fertility treatments it took for her and Sean to conceive. She grew up in Upper Fells Point, a traditionally Irish Catholic neighborhood a short water taxi ride away from Baltimore's Inner Harbor.

"We call it Upper Fells now," Beth clarifies, "but a lot of the older residents, like my parents, still say Fells Prospect."

She and Sean met at a local networking event for young professionals a little over seven years ago.

"It was the typical meet and greet kind of thing, at the Rusty Scupper," Sean recalled. "Maybe a hundred or so people looking for some free appetizers and a drink or two after work."

Sean came to Baltimore from Cleveland.

"It took me three years and a law degree to decide that I really didn't want to be a lawyer," Sean mused.

He connected with a childhood friend who was living in Baltimore and finding some success in the local commercial real estate business.

Sean joined up with his friend at a local firm and has been working there ever since.

"Beth grabbed up the last pig in a blanket from the waiter's tray," Sean recounted. "I made a joke of some kind, she laughed, and we spent the next couple of hours talking and getting to know each other."

"I tell people we fell in love over a hot dog," Beth puts in.

The couple saw each other almost every day for the next several months and got engaged less than a year after they met.

"I was thirty and Beth was twenty-eight. We were both older and had enough of the singles scene," Sean related.

Beth grew up in a large and strict Catholic home, the fourth of six children and the youngest girl in the family. Sean's mother was Catholic, his father more of an atheist.

"His religion was hard work," Sean asserted. "I got a little of the Catholic education when I was younger, but since my dad really didn't care if I went to church or not, I chose not to. I like to call it 'Catholic Lite,'" he said.

"Religion was really everywhere in our house," Beth emphasized; "crucifixes in every room, rosaries, photographs of churches, and other religious symbols were all over the house. And all that we did outside also involved the church: dinners at the rectory, fairs throughout the year, just about everything."

Despite all that, though, Beth's parents divorced not long after her youngest sister left home for college.

"Although divorce is frowned upon, to say the least, none of us kids were surprised," she imparted.

"My parents never really fought. They just didn't talk. Didn't look at each other much. That's what I remember noticing the most. They never really looked at each other, even when they were in the same room. My mom and I sort of drifted apart after I got out of school and went to work."

Beth is much closer with her father and talks with him almost every day. Both she and Sean wanted children.

"We talked about it a lot. Beth came from a big family, I was an only child," Sean explained. "She knew what it was like to have siblings, and I knew about not having them. I wanted my kids to have brothers and sisters—one or the other, both, I didn't care. I just wanted to have at least a couple of kids. Fingers crossed."

Beth smiles at Sean, a big full smile. She leans into him a bit, reaches over, and rests her hand on his knee.

They tried to get pregnant for almost two years without success. Without success on the pregnancy front, the couple got a dog.

"Brownie," said Sean, a Cleveland Browns football fan. "You can take me out of Cleveland, but you can't take the Cleveland out of me."

"We took a little breather, I guess, focused on the pup for a while," Beth concurred.

They started doing research and interviewed a couple of fertility specialists. There was never any hesitation. Both were willing to do whatever they needed to do to have a baby and start a family.

"It was our families that had the hard time," Beth mentioned.

"Not *our* families," Sean stresses, emphasizing the *our*. "Your dad."

"He thought it was unnatural. It didn't fit inside his Catholic view of life and family," Beth elaborated. "I understood where he was coming from but tried to explain that we felt differently, that this could be the only way we would have a family and that we were going through with it, with or without his support. I don't think he ever really got his hands around the idea, but at some point, he became more accepting of it."

"Then he started in with the money—how much it would cost, that we could lose our house, go broke and all that," Sean observed.

"He was worried about me," Beth offered. "He read up on how the hormone injections could cause me health problems."

The couple went ahead with it despite her father's concerns.

"By the time we were into our second treatment cycle," Beth stated, "we had both just about had it."

"With the treatments and each other," Sean added.

Sean struggled with giving Beth the injections. Beth grew frustrated with his impatience.

"Listen, it was all foreign to me. I know they showed us how to do it, but still, I just hated giving you a shot. I was never sure if it was the right place, how far to put the needle in, whether I would hurt you," Sean admitted, looking directly at Beth.

"I know he was anxious about it, but really, it was no big thing. Just do it and we can go on with our day. His nervousness got to be annoying," Beth described.

As frustration mounted, anger started seeping in.

"Finally, I was like, 'Okay, sure, here you go. I have to go to work,'" Sean said. "I would stick her then toss the thing into the trash."

"A syringe," Beth specifies.

"Syringe, yes. I just wanted out of there," Sean declared.

"We seriously were close to the breaking point, I think," Beth shared. "He'd had enough of me, I'd had enough of him. My hormones were raging. I swung back and forth between being sad that I could not get pregnant and angry that he could just go about his life like usual: go to work, have a beer after, play softball on Sundays. I was struggling, and it did not seem like he cared. And if he did care, he didn't notice. That part was probably worse, his being so distant and laissez-faire about things."

As the relationship started to fray, Beth leaned on her Catholic upbringing—and her dad.

"I started reading again. Not the stuff I had to read in Catholic school when I was a kid, books about faith and marriage. And I started talking to my dad a lot," she went on.

"You talked to him every day," Sean points out.

Having accepted her taking the infertility treatment path, Beth's father became a support that proved invaluable not only to her, but to the marriage itself.

"He really helped me. He told me I would get pregnant, not to worry about me and Sean because we loved each other, we were strong and would get through it. But we talked about other stuff, too; just day-to-day things—work, places we wanted to see, just every-day stuff. Talking to my dad was just nice, it was comforting and definitely helped my stress levels. He also got me thinking about how Sean felt about all of this, the male perspective if you will," she reflected.

"I was glad she had some support, talking to her father and all that, but I was still struggling. She thought my getting out of the house would help me get away from the pregnancy situation—so did I, I guess—but it didn't," Sean disclosed. "I thought about it all the time. I missed Beth, missed us, all that sappy stuff. Then it all turned around."

Beth got pregnant.

The couple and both families were excited. "Everyone was over the moon," Sean remembered. "The baby was due the fourth of July, and we were all talking about how cool it would be to have a birthday party each year with sparklers and fireworks."

"God stepped in," Beth said firmly.

"I'm not saying we would have divorced, but we definitely were not in a good place," Sean explained. "The pregnancy got us back to where we were as a couple, and if Beth wants to think that it was God that put a hand on our family, that's okay with me. I'm just not sure why God had to put us through hell before offering that hand."

"He's talking about the miscarriage," Beth articulates. "I woke up one morning at about nine weeks pregnant. My nightgown was wet. I thought I'd had an accident, but when I pulled the blanket up, the entire bed was soaked with blood."

"She screamed, and it scared me to death. I jumped out of bed and called the doctor's emergency line right away. He called back pretty quickly and told us to get to his office when they opened about an hour later," Sean revealed.

"I knew something wasn't right," Beth recounted. "I knew that spotting was not unusual. But that amount of blood. No. It was not right."

Beth had a sonogram as soon as they got to her doctor's office. There was no heartbeat.

"We were both devastated. We stared at the screen. Beth put her hand on her belly. I did too. Beth on the table, me next to her; it was awful," Sean told us.

"He was crying. I was crying. We just could not believe it—all the plans, our future, everything. We had our path; we were happy together and ready to start a family with our baby. Everything was set," Beth imparted. "Then it was gone. All gone."

"That morning through the next day, it was the worst two days of my life," Sean averred. "I will never forget any of it."

"It's all a blur to me," Beth said. "The doctor sent me home, told me to rest and that I would miscarry— bleed it out—naturally. I was all cramped up, crying and miserable. That's about all I can remember."

"I sat with her through most of it," Sean said. "When it was over, I don't think either of us knew what to say. I flushed the toilet and cleaned up and that was it."

"It was a giant hole in our hearts," Beth said, "caused by this person that we never even got to meet."

"You might think that we would have drifted apart, gone our own way after the miscarriage. It was totally the opposite. As strange as it might seem, losing that baby brought us closer. Maybe because we kept a lot of the whole experience to ourselves. We talked about it a lot—just the two of us. There was a lot of crying and a lot of hugging," Sean said.

"And he does not believe it was God's will. Of course it was," Beth avowed. "I don't understand why, but for whatever reason, we were meant to go through that together. That loss helped us to be the couple we are today."

"Again, she can believe what she wants to believe. If it helps her, that's all that matters to me. The bottom line is that it was a horrific experience, something I would not wish on anyone. But we did stick it out together," Sean affirmed.

"We talked instead of watching TV, we took walks and went out to dinners or coffee together—a lot. After a while, we started talking about whether we wanted to try again. I did, but Sean was reluctant," Beth continued.

"I did not want either of us to go through that ever again," Sean emphasized. "I suggested we consider adopting, but Beth wanted to try once more before looking into it further."

"We did the fertility stuff, and it took. I got pregnant. I thanked God every day," Beth related. "Still do."

"We did not tell anyone about the pregnancy until Beth was three months in," Sean noted.

Caroline had her first birthday just a few weeks ago. As an added gift to the family, Beth is pregnant again.

"We weren't even trying. My dad came over and watched the baby. We got dressed and had a lovely night out, Little Italy for dinner and drinks," Beth mused.

"And dessert when we got home," Sean smiled.

No fertility problems this time around.

"My dad is so happy," Beth concluded. "We all are."

OUR TAKE

These two people are clearly on a completely different wavelength when it comes to faith. Beth was firm in her belief that the miscarriage was God's will. She held fast to her faith that there was a plan for her and her family. "Sean, on the other hand, could not understand why God—any God—would take away his baby and put Beth through all the pain she went through—all *they* went through," David commented.

"He accepted her perspective and let it be her perspective. I think there were two strategies at work here," Julie articulated. "The first was Sean's natural sense that Beth should grieve however she had to. Even though he was not buying into it, that was her way. He said something like, 'If that is what she wants to believe and it works for her, then fine.' And the second may have been more of a conscious decision to avoid conflict with Beth."

"If what you are going to say won't matter, then don't say it," David agreed.

Beth found solace and strength in her faith. While Sean did not, he understood that Beth needed that to find some sense in all of it. Most definitely, the couple sustained a loss when Beth miscarried. Is it a different form of loss than with a couple who suffer the loss of a child?

About forty years ago, psychology professor Dr. Pauline Boss published a book titled *Ambiguous Loss*. In its simplest sense, "ambiguous loss" refers to loss without closure. Both infertility and miscarriage fall into that category.

"When Sean and Beth experienced infertility, they essentially went through a grieving process over their not being able to have a baby," Julie clarifies. "Like most of us, both of their brains went to the worst-case scenario—'We can't have kids.' Those thoughts created a ton of emotions—none of them healthy: sadness, guilt, grief, you name it."

"In essence, then, the loss was not knowing if they could have children, and the grief extended over what they thought was an inability to conceive," David reiterated.

"And like I said, both Sean and Beth may have felt guilt as well. There was the uncertainty over whether the loss would continue," Julie went on. "Could they ever have kids? That's the ambiguous part."

The miscarriage is a death. What exactly is ambiguous about that?

"Beth might have been early in the pregnancy, but she still lost their baby; a baby they never got to know and never will know. Boy or girl? Blue eyes or brown? Would she have been good at math like Beth? A million questions never to be answered, just to be wondered about," Julie reflects.

Beth and Sean handled the miscarriage very differently. "Despite her faith, Beth still experienced sadness," David said. "She saw Sean as not feeling the same way, maybe not being sad like she was when of course he was sad—even though he was grieving, too, in his own way, right?"

Sean grieved by keeping busy and did not show the outward emotions that Beth did. Beth also had her father to help give her some perspective on how Sean may have been feeling.

"This is what I mean by 'equifinality,'" Julie specified; "taking separate paths to the same destination. That is exactly what happened here. These two experienced ambiguous loss not once, but twice—losses without closure. Both the infertility issues and the miscarriage caused each of them to grieve. But they did it in different ways."

Beth and Sean were respectful of the contrast between how they dealt with the losses. They stayed together and remained connected, and when the grief process was a bit less raw, they met back up at the same spot—together.

Bulitt Point Takeaways

- Faith can help a couple even if both partners do not hold the same beliefs
- A couple can experience loss in a way that brings them closer together
- If two partners find the same end point, it is fine to take different paths to get there

CHAPTER 15

Tackling Generational Autism

"I have always liked things to be a certain way," Nathan expressed. "To be successful at anything, I believe you need to be organized. And when I say 'anything,' I mean work, marriage, being a parent—everything."

"I could always count on Nathan," Heather remembers. "From the beginning when we first started dating, I noticed it. If Nathan said he was going to pick me up at eight, he pulled in the driveway at eight. Not five of and not five after. Right at eight."

Nathan and Heather have been married for fifteen years. Their twelve-year-old daughter, Sophia, is in middle school and thriving.

"She is terrific," Heather enthused. "Sophia is outgoing, gets great grades, and is just a joy to be around. I know I am her mother, but I am sure her friends' parents would tell you the same thing."

Their eight-year-old son, Charlie, is going into the fifth grade. Charlie was difficult from the start. He did not sleep well, had tantrums, and was very restrictive in what he would eat.

"His behavior was nothing like what we had experienced with Sophia," Nathan clarified. "After a little while, I started to keep a log so that I could remember and accurately report all of his behaviors to our pediatrician. At first, he told us not to worry, but after the behaviors continued, he said Charlie had 'sensory processing' issues and would probably grow out of it."

Charlie did not grow out of it. As he got older and went off to school, the behaviors started to magnify.

"He would get belligerent, refuse to get dressed in the morning. At meals, he would sometimes throw food across the kitchen if he did not like it," Heather described.

"The stomachaches started in preschool. Charlie cried, oftentimes doubling over in pain complaining how bad his stomach hurt," Nathan recounted.

"He never seemed to have any friends. That concerned me," Heather disclosed. "Whenever we picked Sophia up from preschool, she was always playing with at least one or two friends. We had lots of play dates at the local park or little lunches at Chick-fil-A with other parents and their kids. Nothing like that with Charlie. He was usually sitting by himself when we got him from school. The teachers said he was shy, that we should not worry. I did worry. It did not seem normal to me."

By the time Charlie hit second grade, both Heather and Nathan decided that they needed to seek some help and got a referral from their pediatrician to a child psychologist. The testing confirmed what Heather expected.

"By then, I had already been on the internet a bunch of times, trying to figure out things for myself. It was not all that surprising to me that he was diagnosed with being on the autism spectrum," Heather acknowledged. "I watched some show or documentary on cable about kids on the spectrum. After that, I said to myself, that's Charlie. I knew Charlie was autistic."

"The term is 'Autism Spectrum Disorder' to be specific," Nathan added.

"Yes, Nathan," Heather agreed; "Autism Spectrum Disorder. It explained a lot of things: why Charlie never wanted to go places or do things, his having no friends, playing with Legos for hours on end all by himself."

"He was—is—such a picky eater: only peanut butter and jelly sandwiches with the crust off and the bread cut straight across, not on an angle," Nathan recollected. "That and the Kraft macaroni and cheese out of a box. Only the small noodles."

Although both Nathan and Heather were saddened by the diagnosis, they were relieved to know what it was. "The fact that there were therapies, supports, and special programs we could enroll Charlie in where there were other kids who like him were also on the spectrum—it made us feel better," Nathan imparted.

As Nathan and Heather spent more time speaking with specialists and special educators about Charlie and how to help him as he grew older, Heather started to notice some things about Nathan that she had not paid close attention to previously.

"Nathan is an aerospace engineer. He is really brilliant when it comes to math and science. I am sure his IQ is off the charts," Heather affirmed. "But some of his habits, they have always been sort of different. He does not like anything to change. He has driven the same car since we met, and it's not like we can't afford a new one. His socks have to be folded just so and put in the sock drawer the way he wants it: athletic socks on one side, dress socks on the other; lighter colors up in front, darker socks in back. It can make you crazy. Everything that we do is planned and organized. Nothing can ever be in the moment or spontaneous."

"Once we figured things out with Charlie, she started complaining about me a lot," Nathan voiced. "Heather would tell me to look at her when we talked, that it bothered her when she thought I was looking past her or not paying attention. She also got mad after we had sex. I did not think that was nice."

"I love Nathan, and part of what originally attracted me to him was that he was dependable—a sure thing. But it can get boring. And it's not that I don't love him, I do. But there was no kissing, no foreplay, and definitely no passion. Having intercourse in the missionary position for five or ten minutes every couple of weeks is not my idea of a healthy or fun sex life," Heather averred.

It got to the point that Heather no longer was interested in sex with Nathan. "I would do it to make him happy, but I was not really there during sex. I was just looking at the ceiling, waiting for him to finish so I could get back to my book or go to sleep," she remembered.

"I did not really understand why she was mad all the time. I thought she blamed me for Charlie's autism. We knew that Charlie was autistic, and if I was too, there was a good chance he got it from me. Read the research yourself. Autism can be hereditary," Nathan said.

"In a way, I did blame him. I know it's not fair, but I would watch Charlie, all alone in his room building with his blocks for hours on end. Then I saw Nathan at his desk, with his pencils in one cup, pens in another, and markers in a third, with everything on his desk organized just so while he sat in front of his computer all day," Heather elucidated. "I don't know why it took me so long to see it. They were the same."

Heather confronted Nathan with her suspicion that he too was on the autism spectrum. Nathan agreed to go for testing that confirmed the diagnosis. Like his son, Nathan was diagnosed with high functioning autism.

"It used to be called Asperger's Syndrome," Nathan said.

"Once we knew," Heather recalls, "the real question was what we were going to do about it. We were already stressed and spreading ourselves thin taking Charlie to his activities, keeping him engaged, and following the advice of his doctors. There was not a lot of time for us to spend on making our relationship better."

"I wanted Heather to be happy, and I knew she wasn't. I suggested we go to our church pastor and get some advice from him," Nathan went on.

"That was a perfect example of the positive side of Nathan," Heather related. "He came to me one afternoon and said he was sorry for passing along the autism to Charlie. He said that he loved me and wanted us to be a happy family. Then he gave me a typed list of possible things we could do to help our relationship. One of the items on the list was to talk to our pastor."

In their sessions with the pastor, Nathan was again up-front about his being on the autism spectrum. He also took the blame both for Charlie having the condition as well and the damage that had been done to his marriage to Heather.

"It was not just Nathan," Heather concedes. "I knew in my head that that Nathan did not understand why I felt the way I did. Instead of explaining it to him, I did not say anything, and that just made it worse. He did not know the problem, so he could not know what to do to try to make it better. It really wasn't fair of me."

After a few sessions with their pastor, the couple decided to try some counseling with a licensed therapist.

"Our pastor got us started, and he helped us to understand the need to communicate better in order to move our relationship forward," Nathan described. "From there, we felt that we needed other tools and ideas about how to do that, so we went to a marriage therapist."

"She really helped in terms of giving us solid, substantive things we could do to be more communicative and on the same page. Nathan made a daily checklist of what he would do the next day to communicate with me," Heather acknowledged. "He loves checklists, so it was perfect."

"Each night, I made my list for the next day. Usually, it would include a lot of the same things, like to hug

Heather, ask how she was doing, see if I could do her a favor around the house or run an errand for her. I also got a few books on marriage. Some were on sex—how to please your partner. I never really learned about sex, so it was helpful to me to read about what to do and how to do it. Some days, my list included reading a chapter in one of those books," Nathan detailed.

"I did not need lists," Heather explained. "My part was to be sure I explained something clearly to Nathan that he may otherwise have a hard time perceiving due to the autism, like if I needed time to myself or help with Charlie. And I had to tell him in an unemotional way. At first, it was really difficult. I mean, really, most of us react and respond almost immediately during a conversation. I had to train myself not to react, not to tell him to back off or leave me alone. Instead, I had to take a breath, pull Nathan aside, and explain how I was feeling and what I needed him to do. It was exhausting."

"It helps me," Nathan replied.

"I think it is hard work—for both of us. But it's work we are willing to put in because the alternative is not acceptable for either of us," responded Heather, reaching over to hold Nathan's hand.

"I love her," Nathan declared.

OUR TAKE

The two of us talk to so many couples who are on different pages when it comes to parenting their kids. Heather and Nathan stayed on the same page in lockstep in terms of working with Charlie. All of us want our kids to be happy and healthy, to be well-adjusted. It's a real challenge when parents have a child that acts differently than the other kids. Any such diagnosis—here, Charlie's autism—is scary and anxiety provoking. We felt those same emotions over and over again, for years.

"We knew early on when our daughter stuck her head in the oven that something was not right," David revealed. "We laugh about it now, but it was not so funny at the time."

The two of us were often on anything but the same page. "I went right into clinician mode," Julie relates, "attending to what she needs, medications, behavioral therapies, special needs and supports—everything."

David felt differently. "I knew her wiring was off, that there was some sort of mental health diagnosis that we should try to treat. But I also felt—and I still believe—that a lot of what she did, all the oppositional behaviors, refusal to help herself, and constantly blaming others—primarily you—it was purposeful. And by giving her the 'diagnoses'—she didn't have to take responsibility for anything."

There is a lot of contradictory research out there regarding the rate of divorce among parents of special needs children. Some show a higher rate of divorce, others conclude that there is no impact. "If I was guessing, however, I would think that the divorce rate among parents with special needs kids would be higher than those without," David reasoned. "Having a special needs kid adds stress that most relationships can live without. Think about it—potential differences of opinion in terms of how to help the child, going to doctors and other appointments, accommodations at school, extra meetings with psychologists—I could go on and on."

"A real potential breaking point for Heather and Nathan was right after Nathan's diagnosis," Julie imparted. "Many conditions are hereditary, and it is easy to understand why Heather blamed Nathan for passing autism on to Charlie. She understood intellectually that Nathan could not have helped it, but she still felt anger toward him."

"But ultimately, she did not let it allow their relationship to stall," David affirmed. "As we have seen with other couples who hit a roadblock and find a way to get around it, this couple really came together as a team, starting with Nathan's suggestion that they see their pastor and later when they moved over to a therapist."

There is a type of treatment called "Acceptance Commitment Therapy," or ACT. It's psychotherapy that focuses on acceptance and commitment to help increase an individual's psychological flexibility. "I am not sure if this is the type of work that Heather and Nathan did, but it would have been a good fit for them. In ACT, people are invited to open up and express unpleasant and hurtful feelings—such as Heather's anger at Nathan and blaming him for Charlie having autism," Julie added. "The therapist for this couple did really good work. She took Nathan's weaknesses—his rigidity, his need to have order, all of that—and turned it into something that he used to improve his relationship with Heather. She gave him real tools to use in order to improve his relationship with his wife: making lists, the intimacy books—just really insightful mental health support."

At the same time, Nathan deserves enormous credit for using those tools. "This is a guy who was incredibly open to figuring out how to be a better husband and father," David recognized.

"What we see here is a real family team effort—everyone rowing in the same direction," Julie concluded; "both parents helping their son, Heather working to support Nathan, Nathan in turn recognizing his weaknesses and putting in the work necessary to support his family."

Bulitt Point Takeaways

- Assume good intentions
- Autism can be hereditary
- See a mental health professional if you suspect that you or your partner is on the autism spectrum

CHAPTER 16

Managing an ADHD Spouse

Jack sent a text a few minutes before the interview was scheduled to begin. Although the time had been arranged and confirmed several weeks earlier, he and Lily either had to start an hour later than planned or reschedule with us. Electing not to reschedule, the couple finally arrived almost three hours later.

"I hate being late, but I'm so good at it," Jack conceded, laughing as he walked in the door. "It's a joke. Sorry."

"I don't think anyone is laughing, Jack," Lily remonstrated. One step behind Jack, who did not hold the door for her, Lily mimed "I'm sorry" as she followed her husband into the office.

Lily and Jack, who'd then been married for twelve years, met while they were working for the same company in Rhode Island. Jack was in sales, while Lily worked in human relations, primarily handling recruiting and oversight of the firm's administrative staff.

"A lot of hiring and firing," she explains.

Slightly built with cocoa-colored eyes and hair, Lily's posture is firm and straight, as if she is sitting at attention on the couch. When her parents were newly married, they had moved to the American mainland from Puerto Rico and rented a small apartment in Rhode Island. Lily is the oldest of three sisters.

"I never could understand why they went from Puerto Rico all the way up to Rhode Island," Lily recalls. "Quite a difference in weather, culture, everything. My mom and dad were both hard workers, and I think there was plenty of work there. Providence was a nice place to grow up, even if there were not many people of color," she said.

"I moved across the country from Oregon," Jack recounts, his sharp blue eyes beaming. "I really wanted to go somewhere new for college. I like change, new things, always have. And I wanted to try someplace that no one else from my high school would even think about, much less actually attend. My parents were a little sad, as you probably would expect, but they were supportive of me going east. I think they figured I would be back, but I really fell in love with Rhode Island, all of New England really. I graduated in less than four years, got a job, and have not been back to Newberg since."

After dating for three years, the couple moved in together over the objections of Lily's parents. "I just wanted us to be together, but really did not give much thought to getting married," Jack acknowledged.

"My mom and dad were not happy. From their perspective, if you wanted to live together, you needed to get married. At the very least we had to convince them that we were committed to each other and that marriage was part of our plan," Lily went on.

"It was fine with me, sure," Jack articulated. "She told me we had a problem with her parents, and I went right out to the mall and bought a ring—the first one I looked at. It maxed me on my credit card. I went over and talked to Lily's dad, told him that I loved his daughter and showed him the ring."

"A clear benefit of my husband's impulsivity," Lily recognized. "He saw a problem and he took care of it. There was not much thought put into things. He just acted and it all worked out. Of course, he had a big credit card bill that he could not pay, and it accumulated interest at some ungodly rate."

"I know it was impulsive, but I did what needed to be done," Jack replied. "I have always had issues with acting first, thinking later. Half my time in school I think was spent in the principal's office. I am sure I had pretty severe ADHD back then although there was not much in terms of testing for it. I can remember having trouble staying in my seat and finishing just about any assignment that took more than a few minutes. I would usually annoy the teacher or a kid sitting near me, and that also landed me in the principal's office. I was a good talker, though, and usually could weasel my way out of most anything."

"I was totally different," Lily disclosed. "I was the oldest, and both my parents worked a lot. They counted on me to help with my sisters almost every day. I was expected to make sure they did their homework before they could play or watch TV. Some nights when my mom and dad both worked late, it was up to me to get dinner together for the whole family. And they always emphasized getting good grades. I remember this big spelling bee in second grade and all the parents were invited. I

finished second. I still remember the word I missed—
'shudder'—I forgot there were two Ds. My parents
were not happy. Even though I finished better than
eighteen other second graders, it was not good
enough. My dad made me flash cards, and that night
he must have had me spell 'shudder' about two
hundred times."

"I shudder to think about it," Jack said.

"Ha-ha," Lily said. She was not laughing.

"Anyway, my being successful in school was the
most important thing to my parents," Lily averred.

After moving in together in September, Lily and
Jack got married the next spring.

"I saw a lot of issues with Jack during the time
we lived together," Lily recollected. "Not enough
to change my mind, but his problems with time
management and not getting things done—I won't
kid you, they bothered me. He was late everywhere.
All the time. If I did not get him up, he would oversleep
on weekdays and get to work late. There were always
jobs half done, projects that didn't get finished."

Lily and her mom handled all of the wedding plans.

"Whatever she wanted was fine with me," Jack
voiced. "I told her to let me know when and where and
I would be there."

"And I did. I told him when and where about
fifty times," Lily imparted. "I put the date, time, and
address of the church on the chalkboard in our
kitchen and on his nightstand next to his side of the
bed. I left a note in his car. It did not matter though. He
still was almost an hour late for the ceremony. People
thought he was getting cold feet, but I knew that had

nothing to do with it. I can laugh about it now. It was not funny at the time."

Four years into their marriage, the couple had a baby girl. "After I used my leave and Gina was about two months old, I went back to the office. It did not take long for me to realize that I wanted to be home with Gina, being a full-time mom," Lily reflected.

Not surprisingly, Jack was fine with her leaving her job.

"Sure, that's what she wanted, so that's what I wanted. My job was okay, and I figured the money would work itself out. Plus it would be good for Gina to have her mom around all day instead of being plunked with a babysitter or some childcare place."

It didn't take long for Lily to start to become more annoyed with Jack's behavior.

"It was the same thing but worse," Lily revealed. "If I didn't wake him up, Jack would not get to work on time. I needed to do all his laundry, make sure he had breakfast in the morning and dinner at night. We were watching our money, so I had to make him a lunch to take to work. When he came home, it was that 'Disney-dad' thing. A few minutes of playing with Gina and he was off doing something else. It was like I had two kids, not one. And it got to the point that I had really had enough. I did the grocery shopping. I cleaned the house. I took Lily to her play dates and all her doctor visits. I paid all the bills. Oh God, I can't even think what would have happened if I'd left the bills for Jack to handle. It got to the point where I wondered why I even needed him."

"She was distant there for a while," Jack expressed. "Whatever I did was wrong. Anything I said Lily seemed to scoff at, like I was stupid or something. She was sarcastic all the time, and I did not know why she was so angry at me. I was doing what I was supposed to do, what we agreed I would do: work, earn the income for the family. So what if I forgot to finish painting the garage door or forgot to try to fix the bathroom sink? What was the big deal?"

"And that—right there—that was at the heart of it," Lily pointed out. "Nothing was a big deal to Jack. He came, he went, sometimes he paid attention to us, most times he was distracted by something— anything; a football game or some job that he started but of course never finished. It was a big deal."

"Plus she would not have sex with me. That was completely gone. And I was not happy about it," Jack stressed.

"I just was not interested in him sexually. I was tired. Tired of doing everything. Tired of being his mommy," Lily continued.

"Lily made it pretty clear that something had to change, or we were not going to make it," Jack noted. "One morning before work, she handed me my lunch and made it clear that she was thinking about leaving, taking Gina and moving in with her parents."

"I wanted him on some medication. He needed help, therapy maybe. But definitely I thought that medication could help him," Lily said.

"I tried some ADHD medication after college, but it made me feel kind of slow," Jack disclosed. "I was not as productive at work. But I was willing to try again if it meant keeping us together. I went to some therapy, got some medication. What the therapist really helped me with, though, was managing my day. She had me do a weekly schedule each Sunday. It included waking up, what time I would be home, and a block was scheduled to be with the kids and time each day to spend with Lily. I had three hours of exercise built in each week. A half hour of exercise was on my schedule every day but Sunday. Also Lily would tell me what needed to be done around the house or if Gina had a birthday party to go to one day—all of that got put on my calendar. Everything was scheduled. At first, I thought it was a little juvenile, but it helped."

"I saw that he was trying, and that made me happy. For me, I had to stop stepping in and helping him," Lily conceded. "No more micromanaging him. No more setting his alarm clock or waking him up if he was sleeping. That was his responsibility, and Jack knew the consequences if he did not get to work. I told him what things he should put on his calendar, and he did. There were a few slip-ups, but for the most part he stuck to it."

"I started to understand. She was my wife. Not my parent. And that's how she had been feeling," Jack acknowledged.

Lily noticed Jack's efforts and told him how proud she was of him.

"I saw how hard he was working to help our family and make it better at home. The time we had together after Gina went to bed was really nice," Lily affirmed. "It got to the point where I looked forward to getting on the couch with him each night and just talking, him having a beer, me a glass of wine. After a while, the talking turned to more. I wanted him again."

"Our relationship improved, and the sex, well, that was great too," Jack concurred.

"I guess you could say we fell in love again," Lily ended.

OUR TAKE

Jack is a fairly typical person with ADHD. "You heard him—he can remember being in trouble in school, but working his way out of it," Julie points out. That has continued into adulthood and his relationship with Lily. He is a good problem solver, as are a lot of ADHD individuals. He has good social skills; he is charming and friendly—also not unusual qualities for someone with ADHD. He was successful in his career in sales even though he needed Lily to make sure he got to work on time.

"And he operates well under the gun, in a crisis, right? Her mother and father were not going to let Lily move in, so Jack solved it in a flash," Julie reasoned. "He went out and bought a ring right away."

Jack did not stop to ask Lily what she might want in a ring, the kind of stone or the design. "And it was the first ring he saw in the first store he went into," David observed.

When a person dealing with ADHD pairs up with someone who does not have ADHD, that person—

here it was Lily—becomes the one in charge of the family's entire executive functioning responsibilities. Think of a store or office manager. Lily organized everything; she planned everything. It was her responsibility to tell Jack what he had to do, where he had to go, and when he had to be there.

"Lily became overwhelmed. She was taking care of everything. All the family responsibilities were on her plate: kid, house, bills—everything," Julie enumerated. "She became resentful of having to do it all. They both said it. Her relationship with Jack was more akin to a parent and a child, not a partner. And there is nothing sexy about that."

"And believe me, what Jack did to move forward was not easy for someone with ADHD to do," Julie added. Jack has a disability. It took courage to go to the therapist, take the medication, and employ the strategies that the therapist suggested.

"Jack made his daily list and stuck to it. He accomplished things, he spent quality time with the family, he started tasks and finished them. Lily didn't have to wake him up anymore, make his lunch, make sure he was on time," David recognized. "But up to that point, wasn't she just enabling the behavior? I mean, what if Lily did not do those things to begin with? Don't you think Jack might have pulled it together on his own once he realized it was not Lily's job to be his mother?"

The truth is that people who suffer from severe ADHD know what it is they should do but are unable to put one foot in front of the other and execute the task or job. "One client I was working with told me her husband got annoyed with her misplacing her keys," Julie related. "He told her repeatedly, 'Just put them on the hook when you get home. It's not that difficult.' She told him that if it was that easy for her, she would have already been doing it without his asking her over and over again. Same thing here with Lily. What seems easy to many of us just is not for someone with ADHD. She had trouble understanding Jack's disability, and that is why she wanted to pull her hair out."

When Lily saw that Jack was putting in the effort and making progress, she pulled back from managing him and taking on his responsibilities.

"Lily clearly recognized that her doing everything was not good, and yes—that it was enabling Jack's behavior to some extent," Julie clarified. "But like most partners of ADHD adults, she had to be thinking, 'If I don't do it, it won't get done.' Lily did a good bit of reading and learning. She had to work on her perspective and learn new skills in order to really understand and work through Jack's limitations. And I am sure Jack worked hard but also had lots of slip-ups."

"Lily definitely had quite the tightrope to walk," David commented. "She had to sit on her hands and let Jack try to manage things on his own. At the same time, though, she had to be ready to clean up the mess if he faltered."

The payoff for this couple was a reconnection. There was a direct correlation between Jack's decrease in dependency and the increase in Lily's feelings of love and attraction toward him. "Once

Lily's responsibilities lessened," Julie concluded, "Jack became less of a burden and more of what he was supposed to be—a partner."

Bulitt Point Takeaways

- There needs to be an equitable division of responsibilities in a relationship
- Equitable does not necessarily mean equal
- A partner with ADHD requires patience and structure

CHAPTER 17

Preventing a Blended Family from Breaking

Walking a step behind Katie, Bryce bent a little as he entered. Although there was more than enough room and Bryce was not really in danger of hitting his head on the doorway, it was easy to see how the thought may have crossed his mind. Six foot four—maybe five—and built like a Marvel superhero, it seemed fitting that Bryce heads up a local police SWAT unit.

Katie's not exactly chopped liver. Trim and muscular, with a body fat percentage likely hovering just a bit above zero, Katie is a fitness coach and trainer who teaches multiple classes at local gyms.

"Come on in, big guy," Katie encouraged Bryce, waving him in behind her.

The couple first met at a spin cycle class. At the time, both were in the midst of failing marriages, processing through separation and divorce. They connected quickly, finding much in common, starting with their foundation of Christian faith.

"My marriage was soulless," Katie recounts. "I had the kids, but I was lonely for a long time. Our relationship was over well before we got the divorce."

"Mine was dysfunctional from the start," Bryce reflected. "Except for our three kids, there was really nothing else between us. We did not talk or see eye to eye on much of anything."

Katie and Bryce soon began dating and fell in love.

"We were kind of sneaking around," Katie remembers. "Neither of us liked that feeling, and we decided we needed to make it official and tell all the kids."

"It was important to let the kids know what was going on. I wanted to be up-front and get our family started on the right foot," Bryce emphasized. "I didn't want my kids to go through what they went through with me and their mom. I thought it was important for everyone that we build a stable home for our family together."

"Our plan was to move the family into Bryce's house," Katie explained. "But we needed more space for us and the five kids, so we started to work on an addition."

During the course of the construction, they found another house in the neighborhood that they felt would be a perfect fit for the family.

The couple faced an immediate challenge that almost broke them up right from the start.

"We agreed that the other house would work better than where Bryce was living. It gave everyone a fresh start, and that was exciting and fun for everyone," Katie recalled. "What I didn't think through was the school situation."

"We had agreed that all the kids would go to the public schools in our district," Bryce confirmed.

But as the beginning of school came closer, Katie began to have second thoughts.

"I started to panic really. My kids had been in a small Christian school for several years," Katie elucidated. "It was like a second home. It helped my girls to have some stability and security when we needed it. I made a mistake when we decided to move them out of their school. There was a lot going on, and I honestly did not give it enough thought."

Katie changed her mind and told Bryce that her girls were going to stay in the smaller school. Bryce is a planner, a tactical type of thinker who does things in advance. He did not take the news well.

"We talked in advance about all of our plans for the family. That included the schools they would go to. It made sense for all the kids to be in the public schools near the house, for them and for the two of us. Katie agreed," Bryce shared. "The other school was maybe forty minutes away, longer in traffic. Splitting the kids into different schools was going to force both of us to do a lot more driving separately. Between back and forth to schools, activities for all the kids, and us both working long hours, that made for a lot less time for everyone to be together as a family. And that was not what we planned on or what we agreed to."

Ten years after the two married, the school dispute still rankles them both.

"We had an agreement that we both thought was best for the family. Then she changed her mind and that was that," Bryce voiced. "I really had no choice. If I wanted our marriage to work, I had to go along with it."

A whirlpool of outside influences has continually added stress to their relationship.

"Raising five kids in a blended home is not easy to start with," Bryce stressed. "People called us the Brady Bunch, but it never felt much like a TV show."

All the kids have had numerous athletic and extracurricular activities, and one child has experienced some mental health challenges and an eating disorder. Both former spouses remain on the periphery, bringing reminders of the past and sometimes creating new issues. The very nature of Bryce's job itself adds tension and stress for the family.

"We were under some illusion that love would conquer all," Katie mused. "We both realized pretty quick that being in love was not going to be enough. We had to work at it—that, and our belief that God had a plan for us."

The couple made use of pastoral counseling at their church.

"Neither one of us wanted another divorce under our belts," Bryce pointed out. "It helped us understand that we needed to play to each other's strengths. I like structure. It's important for kids. It's important in life. But I had to learn to give up trying to have control over every situation, let Katie and the kids do things their way, then be there after if they needed help. Still, though, if any of the kids are in a jam or need help, I am the one they call."

"He is definitely the one the kids reach out to if there is a problem or if one of them needs some help kind of picking up the pieces," Katie concedes.

"We just have different styles when it comes to parenting," Bryce observed.

"That is for sure," Katie declared. "I raised my girls basically on my own for a long time. I did things my way, and there were no questions or debates about things. With Bryce, I have had to learn how to trust his judgment and back off. It was not easy. Still isn't. But the fact is he is right about 97 percent of the time."

Not that long ago, Katie and Bryce sat the kids down for a talk.

"We apologized to them for a lot of things," Katie disclosed; "for not always being the best in terms of role modeling when it came to communication both between the two of us and with them."

"We recognized that we did not do a great job early on of being clear and consistent in terms of rules for the kids and what we expected of them," Bryce agreed.

"And we told them that we were sorry for thinking that all would somehow magically be fine in a home with five kids, all of whom were starting over and getting to know each other—and believing that all we as parents had to do was be in love and we would have no problems," Katie revealed.

"I think if we had to do it all over again, we would have waited and not put everyone together so quickly. More time getting to know each other and maybe some family counseling at the church would have been helpful," Bryce surmised.

"There were seven of us. All of us had been hurt in one way or another," Katie articulated. "We were strangers in a lot of ways. We should have taken some more time for sure. But it worked out. We made it."

OUR TAKE

Blended families can be tricky.

"There have been a lot of studies of stepfamilies. Basically 60–70 percent of marriages involving children from a prior relationship do fail," Julie imparted.

We have talked about second marriages and marriages later in life being difficult and challenging in and of themselves. Add into the mix the kids, ex-spouses, maybe in-laws and former in-laws, careers, and different habits and ways of doing things.

"It's got to be a lot," David noted. "You are taking two completely separate family units—two ways of living, really—and trying to merge them into one new group under one roof."

There are likely to be issues around the kids seeing the other biological parents, and that can make things more complex. The new couple is trying to establish a new order so to speak with all the kids, but maybe some or all of them also are going back and forth to the other biological parent, where, again, the way of life is different.

"Katie really got it right. Blended families are almost always born out of prior relationship losses," Julie explained. "There were hopes and dreams before, the kids had them and the parents had them. When they broke up, it led to feelings of failure and abandonment, both for the adults and the children. And often, kids—and I mean kids of all ages— often have thoughts and fantasies of their parents getting back together long after they've separated and divorced."

When children see their parent with a new partner who becomes a new spouse, it is natural for them to feel and express anger and resentment. And who bears the brunt of those feelings? All the parents—the stepparents and the biological parents alike.

"The school conflict almost derailed these two early on. For all it seemed they did talk about—their faith, where they would live, and so on—it's hard for me to understand how the issue of schools did not come up," David expressed.

"Bryce made an assumption—a logical one—that the kids would go to schools near their house. As Katie said, she simply did not think it through. She went along with it. Until she didn't," Julie commented.

Did Katie purposely avoid talking about it?

"I don't believe so," Julie asserted. "Katie did not make the decision not to talk about it. They had a lot going on. She and Bryce made the decision that they wanted to 'come out,' as one of them said, and not hide their relationship any longer. They were in love and wanted to get to work building a new family unit. The issues that her girls would face changing schools really did not hit Katie until right before it was going to happen."

Bryce is a guy who thinks things through. He is a planner.

"He had it all worked out until Katie threw a wrench into things and told him that the girls were not going to switch schools," David reiterated. "From my perspective, Katie made two mistakes. The first, as you said, was not intentional. She did not give it enough thought. Fair enough. But when Katie realized that it was a mistake to move the kids out of their school, I think she should have sat down with Bryce and explained to him how important it was for her girls to stay where they were. There is nothing at all wrong with Katie changing her mind. She should have just been up-front about it, and I think Bryce would have understood."

There is a lot to the concept of "It's not what you say, it's how you say it."

"Had Katie come to him, owned her feelings, and told him how concerned she was for her girls, that she was afraid leaving their school would be harmful to them and in turn to the family as a whole, the couple might have avoided the entire conflict," Julie reflected.

Katie and Bryce did not spend much time establishing a relationship foundation that could have helped in terms of getting past the school conflict.

"They definitely did not take the time that many of us do when we are getting ready to build a life together," Julie observed. "At the outset of many relationships, a couple dates and spends a lot of time together, just the two of them. Katie and Bryce had been married already and failed at it. They both had kids that they were trying to parent—often on their own. There was not a lot of time to 'form their base,' so to speak. The two of them jumped in with all of this work to do right off the bat."

We call it the "building" portion of a relationship. Katie and Bryce mostly skipped over that relationship step.

"But look at where they are now," Julie recognized; "the two of them sitting those kids down, talking to them, and owning up to the mistakes they made, acknowledging the way they'd fought, argued, and not communicated well. Really wonderful repair work."

"Being open about what they did wrong and how they might do things differently now: those types of discussions have a great impact on kids. And the two of them were on the same page, they did it together—it was helping to heal a wound from the past."

"It's a spot-on example of what we say in therapy: that we are hurt by people, and we are helped by people," Julie elucidated.

These are both strong-willed, high-energy people. Katie and Bryce not only learned each other's habits, weaknesses, and strengths; they adapted to them. Figuring all that out was not easy, but part of growing as a couple is learning when to let your partner manage or take care of a situation. Certainly, the strong connection through their faith has helped them in that way, as has their faith in each other.

Bulitt Point Takeaways

- Adjust parenting responsibilities so as to take advantage of each partner's strengths
- Communicating shortcomings or failures to your children is an example of both effective parenting and excellent role modeling
- We can be both hurt and helped by others

CHAPTER 18

Adapting and Adjusting
to Gender Transition

"I'm much more of a talker than Andy," Claudia announced as the couple sat down. In her mid-fifties but with a figure that would pass for that of a much younger woman, Claudia was well dressed in a pair of high-waist jeans, heels, and a graphic tee underneath a black leather blazer.

Sporting salt-and-pepper hair, trim, and clearly in good shape, Andy was no slouch in the looks department himself. "She tends to occupy a conversation," Andy concurred. "Has for years."

The two just celebrated their twenty-eighth anniversary at the same bar where they first met. "We were both going through a divorce at the time; we chatted some at the bar. He smiled a lot but did not talk very much. I caught him staring at me a couple of times and at first thought he was a little creepy," Claudia recalled.

"Staring might be a little bit of an exaggeration," Andy voiced. "I noticed her for sure. Who wouldn't? She was gorgeous and I was single, a year out of a lousy marriage," he said.

"I was attracted to him but was hesitant to give him my number. We walked out together, and I just told him how nice it was to meet him. We said goodbye and walked to our cars."

"She took my license plate down," Andy adds.

"I was not taking any chances. I was almost divorced from one controlling jerk when I went right into dating another loser. I did not want to make it three in a row," Claudia disclosed. "So I called a buddy who was a cop and had her run this one's plate. Had a credit check done too."

"I checked out apparently," Andy went on. "She called me, and we agreed to meet up for dinner. I'd never had a woman call me for a date. It was cool. Impressive."

"Things moved along quickly, once I got my security clearance," he laughed. "I asked her to move in with me a few months after we met. It was fast, sure, but it just felt right. We agreed to give it six months. If it was good, we would get engaged. If not, Claudia would move back out."

"It was pretty quick for me, too," Claudia revealed. "My friends thought I was nuts, moving in with Andy so quickly. We worked well together living in the same place. I just did not like that it was where Andy and his first wife had lived together."

"We decided to get engaged before the six months was even up," Andy related. "I found us a house to buy, and we went ahead and made the move. I told her if we broke up at least the place was a good investment."

"Funny guy," Claudia mused. "We got married soon after the move to the new house. Both of us felt like we had catching up to do after wasting so much time with our first marriages. We wanted to have a family, so we got started trying right away. I had trouble getting pregnant, and we went through some fertility treatments. It was so expensive."

"I did not want to spend all our savings working to have a baby and then not be able to give that baby everything I could," Andy expressed.

"Adoption seemed like a better route—more certain and less expensive," Claudia remembers. "We started working with a local agency, filled out all the forms, and had the home study done so we would be approved when a child became available. What we did not expect was to get a call so quickly."

Four months after registering with the adoption agency, a baby was available.

"We thought for sure it would take a while for them to find a child for us, so we did not rush to get things for the house," Claudia explained. "We had nothing, literally. An empty room for the nursery. No crib, diapers, formula."

"No baby clothes, no car seat. Nothing at all," Andy added.

Both families pitched in, and after several trips to Target and the local baby supply store, all was set by the time the baby arrived.

"That first year with Drew was just the best. He was an easy baby. He didn't cry much, ate well, and hit all of his growth markers," Claudia shared. "The two of us made a great team, we really did. We took turns getting up for feedings at night, changing diapers, taking Drew to the pediatrician—everything. We were tired more for sure, but we really loved being parents, and doing so much together made our relationship even stronger."

"When Drew turned one, I turned to Claudia and told her that I thought he should have a brother or sister," Andy imparted.

"He knew from my response that I was thinking exactly the same thing," Claudia offered. "We reached out to the agency again, paid the fee, and got our file updated."

"Another fast one," Andrew laughed.

"Yes, we got a call from our worker at the agency who told us that two premature babies had been born to a young mother. They were set to be adopted, but the prospective parents backed out," Claudia continued.

"They were worried about health problems down the road, I guess, with the babies being born so early," Andy stressed. "They were born on Drew's first birthday. We could not say no."

"We both felt strongly that those girls were meant to be ours," Claudia affirmed. "The birth mom picked us from a lot of potential parents. After 103 days in the hospital, the girls were home."

"It was not as if we went into it with blinders on. Obviously, we knew that adding two infants to a one-year-old child was going to cause changes in our lives. We just did not count on so much change," Andy described.

"The first few years after the girls were born are just a blur, an absolute blur," Claudia emphasized. "I remember watching Andy getting up and leaving for work in the morning and praying that I could make it until he got home at six so I could go upstairs and take a nap."

"It was just a lot. The quiet peaceful home we had before was gone. The girls were needy. Our quiet time as a family didn't exist anymore. Drew was starting to exhibit some behavioral issues, and on top of that, the girls were pretty demanding," Andy recalled.

The babies cried often, did not do well on their bottles, and were frequently hungry. There was no time for the romantic connection that Andy and Claudia had shared from the early stages of their relationship.

"Sex was relegated to nothing more than just taking care of another biological function before one of us passed out," Claudia recounted.

"It was a long dry spell, but thankfully it ended," Andy responded. "Once the twins were sleeping through the night—mostly, anyway—we got back to doing it regularly, once a week. Every weekend for sure."

"And it has stayed that way," Claudia agreed. "It's good for us, and we both still enjoy each other in that way."

"All three of the children had issues as they grew up," Andy recollected. "Drew had trouble focusing in school and staying in his seat. He bothered other kids in class. Getting him to do his homework was really impossible."

"Not just at school, but at home also," Claudia clarified. "Either he could not get started on a project—it could have been a school assignment or a chore at home—or once he started, he would never finish."

Drew was diagnosed with ADHD in middle school and started medication and therapy as well as some executive functioning coaching to help him with organization and tasks.

"Both Lucy and Lainey were shy from the get-go. Neither of them was interested in interacting with other kids, and they stayed to themselves. When I would take them to a park or to a birthday party, they seemed anxious, not wanting to leave my side," Claudia observed.

When they reached their early teens, both girls started cutting themselves.

"That—the cutting thing—was hard for me to see," Andy disclosed.

"They were cries for help, obviously, for both of them," Claudia recognizes. "We had gotten a little help when they were younger, but it was not consistent. When they were teens and the cutting started, we knew they were both struggling. Both started therapy and went on medications. Nothing seemed to help. The anger, isolation, and cutting themselves—it all continued. Then almost out of the blue, one day, Lucy told us that she felt she was in the wrong body."

"She thought she was supposed to be a boy," Andy said. "She told us she'd made a decision. She wanted to live her life as a male."

"We wanted her to be happy. If being a boy was going to make her happy, then it was fine with us," Claudia asserted. "We did not know much about being transgender, what it meant, or what the future would bring for Lucy."

After speaking with both girls' doctors, they decided to send them to a therapeutic boarding school out west.

"It was a lot of money," Andy articulated. "We took out a home equity loan to pay for it. Took us years to pay that loan back."

"Money is money. We could work and make it back eventually. These were our kids. We agreed they were both in trouble and that we needed to do all we could to help them—to try to save them," Claudia pointed out. "They would have died if we hadn't gotten them out and into an environment with the supports they needed. I was sure of it. One of my friends' kids came out as gay and just could not adjust at home. He ended up committing suicide. I was not going to let that happen to our girls."

"I agree with Claudia. It was about them surviving. I had a hard time spending all that money, but it was the right thing to do. We gave up a lot—we drove our older cars and had to forget a planned addition to our house. The only vacations we could afford were going to visit the kids at school—and we really couldn't afford those, to be honest."

Soon after the girls moved into their new school, they got a phone call from Lainey.

"It was a lot like our talk with her sister. She was not happy with who she was and did not feel that God intended her to be a woman. She wanted to transition to a male as well," Andy revealed.

"So our two daughters were going to be our two sons. I remember talking to Drew about it. He was like 'Okay, cool,' or something like that. What to say to our family and friends, though, that was more difficult," Claudia mused. "So we didn't tell anyone anything. The kids were not home, and that made it a lot easier for us. It wasn't that we were embarrassed or disappointed. We just were not ready for all the inevitable questions, ridicule, silence, whatever we would have faced."

"We decided to let people know when we were ready to let them know. Although I don't think we ever actually talked about it."

"Probably not," Andy interjects.

"Definitely not," Claudia declares. "It was an unspoken thing for a good while. It was our family's business, not others'. We did do a lot of praying, though."

"And those prayers were answered," Andy maintains.

"Drew fell in love with Utah when we took him out to those family weekends and moved out there after school," Claudia imparted.

"I am so amazed at Drew," Andy enthused. "The kid could not sit still to do a math problem in school, but he learned and trained to become a master electrician. And he has a girlfriend."

"I would have never guessed it, but the other two—now Luke and Lane—they moved back here. They are in the midst of the hormonal therapy, and both are going to have the surgery at some point," Claudia explains.

"Gender correction surgery," Andy followed up.

"My mom still has problems with their new names, and whether to say they are her granddaughters or grandsons. But it's okay. She is doing her best," Claudia acknowledged.

"Claudia puts a smiley face on it. But let's be honest, it was a hell of an adjustment," Andy voiced. "I mean, my daughters were gone."

"They were not gone," Claudia stresses.

"I know that, I do. But I did feel that way for a bit," Andy expressed.

"We talked a lot about Andy feeling like he had lost his girls," Claudia remembers. "I didn't feel that way and did not think he should either. I tried to empathize with him. That it was a loss, but it was also a gain. And on top of it, those two were the same people. Just happier."

"We still get comments and questions every so often," Andy offered; "things like, 'that must be so hard,' or 'how are you handling it?'—and similar such things."

"We just tell them that there is not really anything to 'handle,'" Claudia states. "They are our kids, and we love them. Whatever makes them happy is really— really—all that matters."

OUR TAKE

Both of these people had difficult first marriages. Claudia and Andy were each looking for the right person and definitely being careful about it.

"Now I know they rushed once things got started, but still it was clear they wanted to be a little more cautious than most of us before jumping into a relationship," Julie commented.

"You think? A background check before a first date seemed a little excessive to me," David answered.

Most of us would agree. But getting some basic information about Andy did give Claudia some confidence that Andy was not going to be like the last two guys she had been involved with.

"I've got news for you," David asserted. "Just because someone sails through a criminal background check and his credit report looks okay does not mean he is the perfect guy."

"They did develop a mutual trust in each other, and if that took a little detective work first, then fine," Julie added. "It worked. Also, what was clear to me is that they truly are partners and were from the beginning. Their relationship house had a solid foundation is what I mean. That is a great start."

Their goals were allied, and they were in sync when it came to a desire to have a family. They were also committed to being fiscally responsible.

"And sex is the glue for them. It keeps them connected. I thought it was really interesting to hear both of them agreeing that they missed it during the 'down period' and promising not to let it happen again," David observed. "It's funny. People talk a lot about how they can't have sex with their partner when there is a lot going on, issues at work, problems in the family, whatever. But these two—except for a short stretch—they made the time to be intimate. Mental health struggles. Kids with special needs. Financial stress. Transgender kids—not one, but two. Stress levels had to be off the charts."

"There was a bit more to it, but I agree that the intimacy aspect of their relationship helped them manage that stress and stay connected. We have seen other couples pull apart during tests and trials, but not these two. They huddled and put their arms around each other," Julie pointed out. "You know what else? I did not hear anything from either Andy or Claudia about blaming the other—despite the fact that they have different ways of communicating."

Claudia is much more verbal and likely to articulate her thoughts or opinions in the moment, while Andy is much more of an "inside the head" kind of thinker.

"Different styles for sure, but it works. These two communicate really well with each other," David emphasized. "Neither of them did what we have seen others do—including you and me. 'You should have listened to me,' 'I wish you would not have done that,' or 'If you had done this then, that would have happened.' None of that."

Although Claudia and Andy did not talk about it much, there is a faith component to their connection. Remember the "we prayed, and it worked" comments? Neither of us, either individually or as a couple, have that faith piece as part of our makeup. We work together for other reasons.

"We don't have the religious connection as neither of us are particularly observant. I think that helped Andy, particularly with the loss he felt when his daughters were not daughters anymore," Julie imparted. "It's another example of an ambiguous loss so many of us experience."

"He said it himself—he lost his daughters, but his children were still there. That was so difficult for him. You could see it in his eyes, hear it in his voice," David reflected. "The other thing I really loved about this couple is how protective they became of their relationship and of their kids. What was going on in their family was their business—it was not for public consumption until they both decided that it was."

"Their prime concern was to support and protect their kids, and neither Claudia nor Andy needed to go talk about it with others," Julie concluded.

They had each other, and that was all they needed.

Bulitt Point Takeaways

- Try to maintain some level of intimacy even during the most difficult of challenges
- Two people in a relationship often do not feel the same way about an issue
- It's often not what you say but how you say it

CHAPTER 19

How About Us?

"Our daughter lives in a tent."

That is the beginning of our final interview—the interview with the two of us. In order to write this book, we asked couples to have a light beamed onto the most private aspects of their relationship, to share their intimacies and hopes, their losses and failures. How could we not do the same?

"I met David at a fraternity party over forty years ago. The next day he called me—actually called me," Julie remembers. "Little did I understand how that call came to represent our life together. Good or bad, David does what he says he is going to do. We know where we stand with each other, even when—particularly when—we don't agree. That direct and up-front way we have had with each other I really think is what helped keep us together during the most trying times in our marriage and with Natalie."

"Natalie is the third of four daughters," David elucidated. "We had our first, Amanda, biologically, then Julie could not get pregnant a second time, so we decided to adopt. We found a biological mother in rural Pennsylvania and adopted Zoe. Two years later, we learned that Zoe's biological mother was pregnant again—she had another child in between—but could not keep this one. At first, I was not particularly excited about having another child—I was happy with two."

"We had the opportunity to adopt Zoe's biological sister," Julie explained. "We had to do it."

"Three years after Natalie, we had Josie," David went on, "the old-fashioned way."

Three of the girls have grown up to be incredibly intelligent, successful, and independent young women. Amanda is married, has three children, and owns her own business.

"Since Amanda was about thirteen, she's wanted to own her own hair salon," Julie recounted. "And now she does. It is a great shop that she and her business partner have built from the ground up. They started with two chairs in a basement and now have this amazing upscale salon and boutique."

"Zoe is a high school history teacher. She loves theatre and the arts and like me can really dig into a good television drama," David related.

Josie is outspoken and carving a path in the world of real estate.

"Jo has some of the best of both of us," Julie described. "She is intuitive like David; she understands people and connects like me. And like both of us, she is a dog with a bone when something needs to get done."

Natalie is the outlier. "We knew early on that she was different. She climbed into an oven, waved a knife at the dog," David said. "There were a lot more, but those are two incidents that stand out."

"From the beginning, we looked at Natalie's behavior very differently," Julie articulated. "She clearly had ADHD, and that was supported by evaluations and testing. I wanted to get her on medications and behavioral plans—do all that we could to help her."

"I was not buying it," David stressed. "Did I think she had some mental health struggles? Sure I did. But to me, every time we kept taking her to another therapist or psychiatrist, trying a different medication—all of it gave her a crutch, an excuse for her bad behavior. Julie talked to Natalie in a very mature way, told her that her brain worked differently and needed some extra help. Julie's intentions were all good and came out of love for our daughter. The unintended consequence of that, to me anyway, was that Natalie could do what she wanted, act how she wanted, and none of it was ever her fault. She never took responsibility for anything, and as a result never put the work in herself that she needed in order to get along with others and find her way in the world. And in a lot of ways, I blamed Julie. I felt—and still do—that not everything has to have a diagnosis or be treated with a pill."

"I would certainly say that our differences over Natalie and how to help her really are the one aspect of our marriage that could have caused us to split," Julie revealed. "That and the financial troubles."

"So, we went through this period that we just did not care what we spent—a new car? Sure. How about those boots you love? Get two pairs. Credit cards got run up, and then on the heels of all of that, we decided to send Natalie to a therapeutic boarding school in Utah. All in, her year in Utah cost us about three hundred thousand dollars," David clarified. "Our savings were gone, as was most of the equity in our house."

"The spending was mutual, but in all honesty, I did blame David a little for our being in that situation. It was not fair, but I did," Julie concedes. "He was the one with a financial head, and I thought that he should have kept us from falling so far in that way."

"After spending a weekend at home for a family visit, we took Natalie to the airport to head back to Utah. She screamed, yelled, and caused a lot of unrest at the gate," David recalled. "The airlines representative told us that she had upset other passengers and they were not going to allow her to board the plane. Natalie kept carrying on and screaming. She threw her pizza at me and took off running. The police caught her and all three of us were escorted out of the airport by a Maryland State trooper."

"That led to a few years of drugging, overdosing, and running away. At this point, we have not seen her in years. She had a baby that—thank God—she placed for adoption. She is homeless and living on the streets somewhere in Pennsylvania," Julie shared.

"It's interesting. I do think that having to face the reality of Natalie being back near home after Utah helped us to refocus our energies on each other, our family, and how to get out of the financial predicament we put ourselves into," David reflected. "At that point, I was past blaming and more in a protective mode. I really felt as if I had done what could to help her, the same for Julie. I turned my attention to keeping my marriage together, protecting my wife and my other kids, and repairing our financial situation."

"We took a lot of advice from a book I read, *The Debt Diet*. We stopped our spending and slowly paid off the debts, got ourselves out from under," Julie remembers. "There were a lot more Saturday night dinners at home and on the couch. We took the kids on trips, but usually to our friends' beach house. We even went on one of those time share vacations where it cost a dollar to stay in a place near Disney for a week."

"We checked in with each other almost every week on the financial side of things, where we were, how we were doing. The communication was key to pulling ourselves up. And we did it," David confirmed. "We paid for three of our kids to go to college, and I was very proud of that. It meant a lot to me that my girls could start their work lives without debt hanging over their heads."

"There was a lot of laughing at ourselves and more than a little inappropriate humor," Julie mused. "We both accepted responsibility for where we were and talked a lot about what we could do to get our family in a better place."

"It was Julie's idea that we sit down each year on our anniversary and set out goals for the year," David acknowledged. "Most of the goals were attainable, some were more aspirational. We would reach some of the annual goals, came up a bit short on others.

We did hit one of those aspirational goals a few years ago when we were able to buy our own house at the beach."

"We may never be the richest people on the block, but neither of us really cares about that," Julie went on.

"Money got made and money got spent," David noted. "But we are in a happy place. We have learned to recognize when one of us needs support, to adapt to each other's weaknesses, when to give each other space."

"That's not to say we don't argue now and again, but usually those arguments are less emotional, less blame and anger. And they pass quickly," Julie imparted.

"I am an expert at saying 'I'm sorry,'" David concluded.

CHAPTER 20

What Can We Take from All of This?

We talk a lot about our "Three C's to a Successful Relationship": communication, connection, and consistency. When we did not communicate, our relationship faltered. When we went our own way and ignored what was going on with the other, our relationship was weakened. When we were inconsistent and not available to the other, when we ignored the other's feelings and opinions, our marriage was in distress. But when we paid more attention, talked more, and connected consistently, we were able to repair some of the damage we had inflicted on ourselves, get closer again, and put ourselves in a better place to move our lives forward.

All of the couples in this book experienced trauma and discord, stretching and fraying of the ties that bind relationships. The similarities that each couple has shown are simple and direct. All of our couples found a way to communicate and connect. A great deal of that was drawn from their faith, their belief in a higher being and a divine plan. These couples ultimately found a middle ground, and even solace, not only in each other but in a strong core belief in God.

Our couples all expressed a need to protect each other, a desire to stay connected and find the best in each other. For some couples, it was sex and intimacy that helped to keep the relationship engine running. Others turned outward for someone to help them find their path and move forward, in therapy, couples counseling, or faith-based support. Each couple found a way to mend and repair the damage and overcome the hardship that the relationship had endured, be it an illness or addiction, infertility or gender conversion, a meddling parent, the uncertainty derived from ambiguous loss, a cheating spouse, or even the death of a child.

"I will take you, to have and to hold, for better, for worse, for richer, for poorer, in sickness and in health, until death do us part. I will love and honor you all the days of my life." We all recognize those words, we are familiar with these vows. Many of us have repeated them ourselves. We also know that saying them is a lot simpler than being true to them. The fact is that not all of us can honor our partner and show them love every day. To be fair, most of us don't. But what these couples and their stories show us is that while on some days we may fall short of those vows and our commitments, that does not mean that the buzzer has sounded and the game is over. There is still time to find our way together, to put in the work to understand each other, to show patience and be respectful of each other. Like the couples in this book, stay strong through the stresses and have the courage to stand up to challenges and fight through the failures. Keep the faith even in the darkest of nights. After all, if they can do it, why can't we?

Afterword

As a therapist and a divorce lawyer, the two of us have had both the honor and privilege of working with countless people over four decades. Although we both tire of the work at times or get angry and frustrated with others, we never take for granted the trust and faith that so many have placed in us. Although none of the couples interviewed for this book are clients, they opened a shade and shared their pain, their sorrows, their joys, and their successes. They did so with honesty and grace. Like us, each of these couples share the same hope for you, our readers—the hope that by sharing their spirit and vulnerabilities, you will find the strength, courage, and optimism to tackle your own challenges. When it comes to relationship struggles, there really is strength in numbers. If more couples were willing to talk about the hard things in relationships, we know that so many others would find comfort in the knowledge that they are not alone and possibly the courage to themselves share their experiences with others. Be vulnerable. Be brave. Start today and share your story at **http://www.thebulitts.com/ourstory**.

About the Authors

Julie Bulitt is a licensed clinical social worker who has spent more than twenty-five years working with individuals, couples, and families. Her private practice focuses on family, couples and individual therapy, ADHD, and executive functioning coaching. She has served as a Clinical Supervisor and Early Childhood Mental Health Consultant for the Montgomery County (Maryland) Mental Health Association, and as an Adoption Therapist for the Center for Support and Education in suburban Washington, DC. She presently serves as the in-house therapist for The Discovery Channel in Silver Spring, Maryland.

David Bulitt is a partner in the Washington, DC, Metro law firm of Joseph, Greenwald & Laake, PA. For more than a decade, he has been chosen as one of the area's top divorce lawyers by multiple publications and recognized as one of the "Best Lawyers in America" and a Washington, DC, Metro "Super Lawyer." Praised as "the lawyer who epitomizes stability and old-fashioned common sense" by *Bethesda Magazine*, David has a particular interest in families with special needs children as a result of his personal experiences. He is the author of two fiction novels and multiple articles in legal publications and has appeared on several local shows.

David and Julie have been married for more than thirty-five years. They have four daughters, two of whom are biological and two adopted, three grandchildren, and a golden retriever. They divide their time between suburban Washington, DC, and Bethany Beach, Delaware. Learn more about David and Julie at www.thebulitts.com. They are active on all major social media platforms and can be found @ thebulitts on Facebook, Instagram, LinkedIn, Twitter, and You Tube.

Mango Publishing, established in 2014, publishes an eclectic list of books by diverse authors—both new and established voices—on topics ranging from business, personal growth, women's empowerment, LGBTQ+ studies, health, and spirituality to history, popular culture, time management, decluttering, lifestyle, mental wellness, aging, and sustainable living. We were named 2019 *and* 2020's #1 fastest-growing independent publisher by *Publishers Weekly*. Our success is driven by our main goal, which is to publish high-quality books that will entertain readers as well as make a positive difference in their lives.

Our readers are our most important resource; we value your input, suggestions, and ideas. We'd love to hear from you—after all, we are publishing books for you!

Please stay in touch with us and follow us at:

Facebook: Mango Publishing
Twitter: @MangoPublishing
Instagram: @MangoPublishing
LinkedIn: Mango Publishing
Pinterest: Mango Publishing
Newsletter: mangopublishinggroup.com/newsletter

Join us on Mango's journey to reinvent publishing, one book at a time.